FEAR

37

NOTS

Tami J. Whitmore

Other books by Tami J. Whitmore

Meadowlark Park

The Bluebird House

Advance praise for *37 Fear Nots*:

"Your choice of a book to send me was very interesting. I went in for a biopsy on Wednesday and got some test results yesterday. They didn't find cancer but they found a-typical cells. Now they want to do some exploratory surgery. I know what you mean about leaning on Our Lord. He has always been with me through all of life's trials and tribulations. I don't know why we worry, guess it is our unbelief, like Thomas said. God sent your devotional to me at a perfect time."

Jan

"We got your devotional in the mail and are definitely going to use it! How awesome! We know it will be a blessing and help to us in the coming days."

Bridget

"I had surgery last week and just days before I went in I came across your devotional. I read in there about your experiences with surgery and it helped prepare me."

Linda

Review for *Meadowlark Park*:

"I just wanted to tell you I had the good fortune to read your book, *Meadowlark Park*. What a delight and so beautifully done. It is truly enchanting. I wish my mother were still alive to read it—she loved stories about birds and animals talking. The pretty photos and inspiring and appropriate Bible verses for each story were a wonderful touch. Your work both draws our eyes to God and His magnificent creation and delights our souls as it puts a smile on our faces."

Gayle

Scriptures marked NIV ®are taken from the Holy Bible, New International Version ®, Copyright © 1973, 1978, 1984, 2011 by Biblica, Inc. Used by permission. All rights reserved worldwide.

Scriptures marked KJV® are taken from the Holy Bible, King James Version®, Copyright© 1982 by Thomas Nelson. Used by permission. All rights reserved.

Scriptures marked NKJV ® are taken from the Holy Bible, New King James Version®, Copyright © 1982 by Thomas Nelson. Used by permission. All rights reserved.

All poems and songs not in public domain used by permission.

Composition/Song Title: "COME HOME"
Writer Credits: Wayne Watson & Michael Omartian.
Copyright: © 1998 Material Music (administrated by Music Services)/Mandipher Music.
All Rights Reserved. ASCAP

37 FEAR NOTS
Copyright© 2016 by Tami J. Whitmore
Published by Create Space
www.createspace.com
ISBN-13: 978-1530125319
Available on www.amazon.com

All rights reserved. No part of this publication may be reproduced, stored in a retrieval system, or transmitted in any form or by any means—electronic, mechanical, digital, photocopy, recording, or any other—except for brief quotations in printed reviews, without the prior permission of the publisher.

This book is dedicated

To the memory of

Timm Butler

(1954-2010)

Table of Contents

Foreward ---9

37. **God is Number One**—*Genesis 21:17*—Hagar & Ishmael---10
36. **Pray For Others**—*Genesis 26:2*—Isaac & Abimelech---14
35. **No Pain**—*Genesis 46:3*—Jacob & Joseph---18
34. **Step of Faith**—*Exodus 14:13*—Moses & Pharaoh---22
33. **God's Daily Care**—*Numbers 14:9*—Joshua & Caleb---26
32. **Sharing Jesus**—*Deuteronomy 20:3*—Moses & Canaanites---30
31. **A Place to Stay**—*Deuteronomy 31:6*—Life & Death---34
30. **Safe in His Arms**—*Deuteronomy 31:8*—Joshua & Moses---38
29. **Do Unto Others**—*Joshua 8:1*—Joshua & Ai---42
28. **Satan is the Loser**—*Joshua 10:25*—Five Kings---46
27. **Why Me, Lord?**—*Judges 6:10*—Gideon & Midian---50
26. **The Lord is Peace**—*Judges 6:23*—Gideon & Baal---54
25. **I Choose Joy**—*2 Kings 25:24*—Jerusalem & Babylon---58
24. **Time is Precious**—*1 Chronicles 28:20*—David & Solomon---62
23. **God is On My Side**—*2 Chronicles 20:17*—Jehoshaphat & Moab---66
22. **Cry to the Lord**—*Psalm 118:6*—Thanks & Love---70
21. **Trust in the Lord**—*Proverbs 3:25*—Wisdom & Trust---74
20. **Wait Upon the Lord**—*Isaiah 7:4*—Ahab & Isaiah---78
19. **Be Not Dismayed**—*Isaiah 41:10*—Israel & Jacob---82
18. **He Will Help**—*Isaiah 41:14*—Poor & Needy---89
17. **I Am With You**—*Isaiah 43:5*—Holy One & Savior---93

16. **The Chosen**—*Isaiah 44:2*—Alpha & Omega---99
15. **No Other Gods**—*Isaiah 44:8*—King & Redeemer---103
14. **Everlasting Salvation**—*Isaiah 51:7*—Zion & Eden---107
13. **Future Glory**—*Isaiah 54:4*—Noah & Flood---111
12. **Righteousness**—*Isaiah 54:14*—Tyranny & Terror---115
11. **Freedom**—*Jeremiah 4:9*—Jeremiah & Gedaliah---119
10. **God's Answer**—*Joel 2:21*—Good Medicine---123
9. **A Blessing**—*Zechariah 8:13*—Seeds & Vines---127
8. **Day of Judgment**—*Malachi 3:5*—Gold & Silver---131
7. **Birth of Jesus**—*Matthew 1:20*—Joseph & Mary---135
6. **Kill the Body**—*Matthew 10:28*—Jesus & Disciples---139
5. **Worth More**—*Matthew 10:31*—Teacher & Student---143
4. **Back to Life**—*Luke 8:50*—Jairus & Daughter---147
3. **Fear God**—*Luke 12:7*—Mary & Jesus---151
2. **About Life**—*Luke 12:32*—Labor & Spin---155
1. **Home!**—*John 12:15*—Hosanna!---159

Afterward---163

God Said, "Fear not"---164

Biographies of Quote People---166

Complete List of all the "Fear nots"---182

From Genesis to Revelation---191

My Favorite "Fear not"---192

Author's Note---193

Foreward

During a period of twelve months I went through two major surgeries and also found out that I had skin cancer. I noticed that each time I was faced with one of these health issues, I went through a process, almost like grieving, to reach a point of **"fearing not."**

One week before my first surgery, a friend from church came to me with these words, **"fear not."** At home, I looked up the phrase in *Strong's Exhaustive Concordance* and found that there are actually 37 verses that start with these very words in the King James Version.

As I was preparing for my second surgery, this same friend and I were talking and I said that maybe I should write down each verse and what I felt as "the day" approached—the process I went through. She suggested making it like a devotional (thanks, Bridget!).

So if you're holding this book, go back 37 days before your scary event and count down with me to "the day" you are dreading and remember-------**God said, "Fear not!"**

--Tami J.

FEAR NOT

#37

GOD IS NUMBER ONE

"Whatever you fear most, has no power—it is your fear that has the power."

Oprah Winfrey

Hagar & Ishmael

Genesis 21:8-21 (NKJV)

So the child grew and was weaned. And Abraham made a great feast on the same day that Isaac was weaned. And Sarah saw the son of Hagar the Egyptian, who she had borne to Abraham, scoffing. Therefore she said to Abraham, "Cast out this bondwoman and her son; for the son of this bondwoman shall not be heir with my son, namely Isaac."

And the matter was very displeasing in Abraham's sight because of his son. But God said to Abraham, "Do not let it be displeasing in your sight because of the lad or because of your bondwoman. Whatever Sarah has said to you, listen to her voice; for in Isaac your seed shall be called. Yet I will also make a nation of the son of the bondwoman, because he is your seed."

So Abraham rose early in the morning, and took bread and a skin of water; and putting it on her shoulder, he gave it and the boy to Hagar, and sent her away. Then she departed and wandered in the Wilderness of Beersheba. And the water in the skin was used up, and she placed the boy under one of the shrubs. Then she went and sat down across from him at a distance of about a bowshot; for she said to herself, "Let me not see the death of the boy." So she sat opposite him and lifted her voice and wept.

And God heard the voice of the lad. Then the angel of God called to Hagar out of heaven, and said to her, "What ails you, Hagar? **Fear not***, for God has heard the voice of the lad where he is. Arise, lift up the lad and hold him with your hand, for I will make him a great nation."*

Then God opened her eyes, and she saw a well of water. And she went and filled the skin with water, and gave the lad a drink. So God was with the lad; and he grew and dwelt in the wilderness, and became an archer. He dwelt in the Wilderness of Paran; and his mother took a wife for him from the land of Egypt.

**For the whole story of Hagar and how she came to have Abraham's child,
please read Genesis 16.**

God is Number One

And God heard the voice of the lad; and the angel of God called to Hagar out of Heaven, and said unto her: "What aileth thee, Hagar? FEAR NOT; for God hath heard the voice of the lad where he is."
Genesis 21:17(KJV)

Abraham didn't even give Hagar any money when she had to leave (because of Sarah's jealousy). Just food and water for her and his firstborn son, Ishmael. Where could she go—what was she to do?

"Then God opened her eyes, and she saw a well of water." (vs. 19, NKJV).

"So God was with the lad; and he grew and dwelt in the wilderness" (vs. 20, NKJV).

God is always there, even when people fail you.

I found that out going through this. Basically I had to go through it with just God and me. Oh, I talked about all of the details with family and friends, but the real "inside" stuff was with God. Isn't that the way it should be with everything?

When I was first married, I used to wonder how I could love God more than my husband. But, over the years, I have learned that when Jack is having a struggle of his own, or a bad day, and I need him to help me with something or listen to me, he isn't always able to do it. Because he is human. I've heard it said that Jesus was 100% man and 100% God when he was on this earth.

But God is not human. He is God, and He is perfect, and He is always there and able to help.

I think that's the key to a good marriage; realizing that your mate can't be everything to you. Always share what you can and try to work things out together. But, remember that God can help anytime, whenever you need it, and He is Number One above everyone else. Talk to Him now. Tell Him every fear and He will hear and help.

Genesis 21:17

And God heard the voice of the lad. Then the angel of God called to Hagar out of heaven, and said to her, "What ails you, Hagar? FEAR NOT, for God has heard the voice of the lad where he is." (NKJV)

Don't Quit

When things go wrong, as they sometimes will,
When the road you're trudging seems all up hill,
When the funds are low and the debts are high,
And you want to smile, but you have to sigh,
When care is pressing you down a bit,
Rest, if you must—but don't you quit!

Life is queer with its twists and turns,
As everyone of us sometimes learns,
And many a failure turns about
When he might have won had he stuck it out;
Don't give up, though the pace seems slow—
You might succeed with another blow.

Often the goal is nearer than
It seems to a faint and faltering man,
Often the struggler has given up
When he might have captured the victor's cup.
And he learned too late, when the night slipped down,
How close he was to the golden crown.

Success is failure turned inside out—
The silver tint of the clouds of doubt—
And you never can tell how close you are,
It may be near when it seems afar;
So stick to the fight when you're hardest hit—
It's when things seem worst that you mustn't quit.

Author Unknown

FEAR NOT

#36

PRAY FOR OTHERS

"Confronting your fears and allowing yourself the right to be human can make you a more productive person."

Dr. David M. Burns

Isaac & Abimelech

Genesis 26:16-31 (NIV)

Then Abimelech said to Isaac, "Move away from us; you have become too powerful for us."

So Isaac moved away from there and encamped in the Valley of Gerar and settled there. Isaac reopened the wells that had been dug in the time of his father Abraham, which the Philistines had stopped up after Abraham died, and he gave them the same names his father had given them.

Isaac's servants dug in the valley and discovered a well of fresh water there. But the herdsmen of Gerar quarreled with Isaac's herdsmen and said, "The water is ours!" So he named the well Esek, because they disputed with him. Then they dug another well, but they quarreled over that one also; so he named it Sitnah, which means opposition. He moved on from there and dug another well, and no one quarreled over it. He named it Rehoboth, saying, "Now the Lord has given us room and we will flourish in the land."

From there he went up to Beersheba. That night the Lord appeared to him and said, "I am the God of your father Abraham. **Do not be afraid***, for I am with you; I will bless you and will increase the number of your descendants for the sake of my servant Abraham."*

Isaac built an altar there and called on the name of the Lord. There he pitched his tent, and there his servants dug a well.

Meanwhile, Abimelech had come to him from Gerar, with Ahuzzath his personal adviser and Phicol the commander of his forces. Isaac asked them, "Why have you come to me, since you were hostile to me and sent me away?"

They answered, "We saw clearly that the Lord was with you; so we said, 'There ought to be a sworn agreement between us'—between us and you. Let us make a treaty with you that you will do us no harm, just as we did not molest you but always treated you well and sent you away in peace. And now you are blessed by the Lord."

Isaac then made a feast for them, and they ate and drank. Early the next morning the men swore an oath to each other. Then Isaac sent them on their way, and they left him in peace.

For the story of the famine that caused Isaac to move to Gerar, please read Genesis 26:1-15.

Pray for Others

And the Lord appeared unto Isaac the same night and said: "I am the God of Abraham thy father: FEAR NOT, for I am with thee, and will bless thee, and multiply thy seed for my servant Abraham's sake." Genesis 26:24 (KJV)

Have you ever been awakened in the middle of the night and sat straight up in bed with a pounding heart, "scared to death"? Yes? Well, I have many times, not the least of which was during those pre-surgery times. It usually took a few hours for me and the Lord to get me calmed down.

But once I was a little settled, and before I went back to sleep, I discovered that this was a marvelous time to pray.

Not just for myself, but for others as well.

I once heard of someone who asked the Lord this question: "Why do your people have so many needs these days?" And He answered this way: "It is not that there are more needs, it is that you are caring for others more."

I was very shy for many years. Then one day I realized I would never get to know more people until I forced myself to go up to them and talk.

So, I did.

And I really began to enjoy myself. It is amazing how people will unburden themselves if you just take the time to listen.

Shortly after this, someone came up to me and said, "I am impressed at how easily you talk with people! It must be a gift. I wish I could do that." And so I shared with her my discovery.

There is always someone (actually, a lot of someones) with many more troubles than we can even imagine. Pray for them and know that some of them are probably praying for you.

Genesis 26:24

And the Lord appeared to him the same night and said, "I am the God of your father Abraham; DO NOT FEAR, for I am with you. I will bless you and multiply your descendants for my servant Abraham's sake." (NKJV)

Sweet Hour of Prayer

Sweet hour of prayer, sweet hour of prayer, that calls me from a world of care,
And bids me, at my Father's throne, make all my wants and wishes known!
In seasons of distress and grief, my soul has often found relief,
And oft escaped the tempter's snare by thy return, sweet hour of prayer.

Sweet hour of prayer, sweet hour or prayer, thy wings shall my petition bear
To Him, whose truth and faithfulness engage the waiting soul to bless;
And since He bids me seek His face, believe His word and trust His grace,
I'll cast on Him my every care, and wait for thee, sweet hour of prayer.

Sweet hour or prayer, sweet hour of prayer, may I Thy consolation share,
Till from Mount Pisgah's lofty height I view my home, and take my flight;
In my immortal flesh I'll rise to seize the everlasting prize,
And shout while passing through the air, farewell, farewell, sweet hour of prayer!

William W. Walford (1772-1850) was born in England and became a popular preacher. Although blind, he was able to quote vast amounts of Scripture from the Psalms, the New Testament, the Prophets and some of the Histories of the Bible. He had no formal education, but in 1845, this poem appeared in the New England Observer and was soon set to music by William B. Bradbury. It is a well-known hymn yet today. The reason he references Mount Pisgah is because that was the mountain from which Moses had his first view of the Promised Land. In Walford's case, his meaning is his first view of Heaven.

FEAR NOT

#35

NO PAIN

"Courage is fear that has said its prayers."

Dorothy Bernard

Jacob & Joseph

Genesis 45:25-28 (NKJV)

Genesis 46:1-7 & 28-30 (NKJV)

Then they went up out of Egypt, and came to the land of Canaan to Jacob their father. And they told him saying, "Joseph is still alive and he is governor over all the land of Egypt." And Jacob's heart stood still, because he did not believe them.

But when they told him all the words which Joseph had said to them, and when he saw the carts which Joseph had sent to carry him, the spirit of Jacob their father revived.

Then Israel (Jacob) said, "It is enough. Joseph my son is still alive. I will go and see him before I die."

So Israel took all that he had and started his trip. He went to Beersheba, where he offered sacrifices to the God of his father Isaac. During the night God spoke to Israel in a vision and said, "Jacob! Jacob!"

And Jacob answered, "Here I am."

Then God said, "I am God, the God of your father. **Don't be afraid** *to go to Egypt, because I will make your descendants a great nation there. I will go to Egypt with you, and I will bring you out of Egypt again. Joseph's own hands will close your eyes when you die."*

Then Jacob left Beersheba. The sons of Israel loaded their father, their children, and their wives in the wagons the king of Egypt had sent. They also took their farm animals and everything they had gotten in Canaan. So Jacob went to Egypt with all his descendants--his sons and grandsons, his daughters and granddaughters. He took all his family to Egypt with him.

Then he sent Judah before him to Joseph, to point out before him the way to Goshen. And they came to the land of Goshen. So Joseph made ready his chariot and went up to Goshen to meet his father Israel; and he presented himself to him, and fell on his neck and wept on his neck a good while.

And Israel said to Joseph, "Now let me die, since I have seen your face, because you are still alive."

For the story of how Joseph became a slave in Egypt, please read Genesis 37.

No Pain

And He said, "I am God, the God of thy father: FEAR NOT to go down to Egypt; for I will there make of thee a great nation." Genesis 46:3 (KJV)

I was ill before my first surgery. When I went for my yearly physical, my doctor immediately scheduled tests for the next day. His office kept calling me and informing me how anemic I was and cautioned me not to drive, do housework or even be alone at home.

By the third day, I was in the office of a specialist; the one who would ultimately perform the surgery. As you can imagine, by this time I was a bit rattled and overwhelmed, and yes, afraid.

I thought that maybe I was going to have emergency surgery in a few days and I hadn't gone through the *37 Fear Nots* yet! Actually, I hadn't even discovered them at this point.

Anyway, with all of this swirling around in my brain, I went to see the specialist. We began to talk and he said that he needed to perform a test that was very painful. He was just letting me know so that I could prepare myself for it (he is a Christian man).

I wasn't sure how to "prepare myself," but I did know that I needed some time alone with God.

So, I asked to be excused to go to the bathroom.

That little room became the place of panic-praying. The last three days had been very frightening and I was at the end of my rope.

But, remember, God is always there and ready to share with us all of His strength that we need.

The procedure was done and there was absolutely no pain. The doctor was amazed and asked if he could take another sample. Again, no pain. I shared about my praying and he agreed that it does help, but still shook his head in wonderment. I have since talked with other women who underwent the same procedure, and those who prayed had no pain.

Genesis 46:3

So he said, "I am God, the God of your father; DO NOT FEAR to go down to Egypt, for I will make of you a great nation there." (NKJV)

It Couldn't Be Done

Somebody said that it couldn't be done,
But he with a chuckle replied
That "maybe it couldn't," but he would be the one
Who wouldn't say so till he'd tried.
So he buckled right in with the trace of a grin
On his face. If he worried he hid it.
He started to sing as he tackled the thing
That couldn't be done, and he did it.

Somebody scoffed: "Oh, you'll never do that;
At least no one ever has done it";
But he took off his coat and he took off his hat,
And the first thing we knew he'd begun it.
With a lift of his chin and a bit of a grin,
Without any doubting or quiddit,
He started to sing as he tackled the thing
That couldn't be done, and he did it.

There are thousands to tell you it cannot be done,
There are thousands to prophesy failure;
There are thousands to point out to you, one by one,
The dangers that wait to assail you.
But just buckle in with a bit of a grin,
Just take off your coat and go to it;
Just start to sing as you tackle the thing
That "cannot be done," and you'll do it.

Edgar Albert Guest (1881-1959) was known as the *People's Poet* after he immigrated to America from England. He started as a copy boy at *Detroit Free Press* and was a reporter when his first poem was printed at the age of 17. During his lifetime he wrote over 11,000 cheerful poems that were syndicated in over 300 newspapers and compiled into 20 books.

FEAR NOT

#34

STEP OF FAITH

"'Fearless' is living in spite of those things that scare you to death."

Taylor Swift

The Red Sea

Exodus 14:10-28 (NIV)

As Pharaoh approached, the Israelites looked up, and there were the Egyptians, marching after them. They were terrified and cried out to the Lord. They said to Moses, "Was it because there were no graves in Egypt that you brought us to the desert to die? What have you done to us by bringing us out of Egypt? Didn't we say to you in Egypt, 'Leave us alone; let us serve the Egyptians'? It would have been better for us to serve the Egyptians than to die in the desert!"

*Moses answered the people, "**Do not be afraid**. Stand firm and you will see the deliverance the Lord will bring you today. The Egyptians you see today you will never see again. The Lord will fight for you; you need only to be still."*

Then the angel of God, who had been traveling in front of Israel's army, withdrew and went behind them. The pillar of cloud also moved from in front and stood behind them, coming between the armies of Egypt and Israel. Throughout the night the cloud brought darkness to the one side and light to the other side; so neither went near the other all night long.

Then Moses stretched out his hand over the sea, and all that night the Lord drove the sea back with a strong east wind and turned it into dry land. The waters were divided, and the Israelites went through the sea on dry ground, with a wall of water on their right and on their left.

The Egyptians pursued them, and all Pharaoh's horses and chariots and horsemen followed them into the sea. During the last watch of the night the Lord looked down from the pillar of fire and cloud at the Egyptian army and threw it into confusion. He made the wheels of their chariots come off so that they had difficulty driving. And the Egyptians said, "Let's get away from the Israelites! The Lord is fighting for them against Egypt."

Then the Lord said to Moses, "Stretch out your hand over the sea so that the waters may flow back over the Egyptians and their chariots and horsemen." Moses stretched out his hand over the sea, and at daybreak the sea went back to its place. The Egyptians were fleeing toward it, and the Lord swept them into the sea. The water flowed back and covered the chariots and horsemen—the entire army of Pharaoh that had followed the Israelites into the sea. Not one of them survived.

For the story of how the Israelites left Goshen, please read Exodus 7-12.

Step of Faith

And Moses said unto the people: "FEAR YE NOT, stand still, and see the salvation of the Lord, which He will shew to you today: for the Egyptians whom you have seen today, ye shall see them again no more forever." **Exodus 14:13 (KJV)**

So, they said that I needed surgery and I signed all kinds of papers releasing them from liability, and agreeing to the procedures of the operation. At first, you're relieved to know you're not a baby; something really is wrong, and they need to fix it.

Okay, that's great. Let's get this thing taken care of because I'm tired of living this way.

Yes, yes, yes on all of the forms.

Hey! What am I doing? I don't know what's going to happen. I don't know what this is going to feel like. I don't know if it will be better after than before—HELP!

I remember, that between my two surgeries, my sister-in-law asked me to go over every single detail of my first experience because she was having the same, and wanted to be informed.

Well, she was so "informed" she couldn't sleep that night!

I think surgery is a lot like childbirth. Going through it is awful and you say to yourself, "Why am I doing this?" Afterwards, everything is all wonderful again and you think; it wasn't that bad after all.

Then your husband says, "If I was you, I'd never want to do that again!" But we do.

I talked with someone who had had my same experience and they said that I would be so glad that I did it—it would be wonderful. Well, it is wonderful now, but going through it was a step of faith **and it hurt.**

All I know is; we took it one day at a time, never knowing how much pain there would be or what complications would arise. Just stepping out in faith every single day, come what may.

Exodus 14:13

And Moses said to the people, "DO NOT BE AFRAID. Stand still, and see the salvation of the Lord, which he will accomplish for you today. For the Egyptians whom you see today, you shall see again no more forever." **(NKJV)**

Faith of Our Fathers

Faith of our fathers living still, in spite of dungeon, fire and sword,

O how our hearts beat high with joy whenever we hear that glorious word!

Our fathers, chained in prisons dark, were still in heart and conscience free:

How sweet would be their children's fate, if they, like them, could die for Thee!

Faith of our fathers, we will love, both friend and foe in all our strife:

And preach Thee, too, as love knows how, by kindly words and virtuous life.

Faith of our fathers,

Holy faith.

We will be true to thee to death!

Frederick William Faber (1814-1863) is known for his many hymns as well as poetry collections. His childhood was spent in Westmorland and he attended college at Oxford. He won the Newdigate Prize (also won by Oscar Wilde) for his poem, *"The Knights of St. John"* and was elected to the National Scholars Foundation. After being appointed Rector at Elton church, he later joined John Henry Cardinal Newman (#11 in our Biography section) and lived and served at Newman College for many years.

FEAR NOT

#33

GOD'S DAILY CARE

"Nothing in life is to be feared, it is only to be understood."

Marie Curie

Joshua & Caleb

Numbers Chapters 13 & 14 (NIV)

The Lord said to Moses, "Send some men to explore the land of Canaan, which I am giving to the Israelites. From each ancestral tribe send one of its leaders." So, at the Lord's command Moses sent them out from the Desert of Paran: from the tribe of Judah, Caleb son of Jephunneh; from the tribe of Ephraim, Hoshea (Joshua) son of Nun.

So they went up and explored the land. When they reached the Valley of Eshcol, they cut off a branch bearing a single cluster of grapes. Two of them carried it on a pole between them, along with some pomegranates and figs. At the end of 40 days they returned from exploring the land.

They came back to Moses and Aaron and the whole Israelite community at Kadesh in the Desert of Paran. There they reported to them and to the whole assembly and showed them the fruit of the land. They gave Moses this account: "We went into the land to which you sent us, and it does flow with milk and honey! Here is its fruit. But the people who live there are powerful, and the cities are fortified and very large. We even saw descendants of Anak (giants) there."

Then Caleb silenced the people before Moses and said, "We should go up and take possession of the land, for we can certainly do it." But the men who had gone up with him said, "We can't attack those people; they are stronger than we are." And they spread among the Israelites a bad report about the land they had explored.

That night all the people of the community raised their voices and wept aloud. All the Israelites grumbled against Moses and Aaron, and the whole assembly said to them, "If only we had died in Egypt! Or in this desert! Why is the Lord bringing us to this land only to let us fall by the sword? Our wives and children will be taken as plunder. Wouldn't it be better for us to go back to Egypt?"

Joshua son of Nun and Caleb son of Jephunneh, who were among those who had explored the land, tore their clothes and said to the entire Israelite assembly, "The land we passed through and explored is exceedingly good. If the Lord is pleased with us, He will lead us into that land, a land flowing with milk and honey, and will give it to us. Only do not rebel against the Lord. And do not be afraid of the people of the land, because we will swallow them up. Their protection is gone, but the Lord is with us. **Do not be afraid**.*" But the whole assembly talked about stoning them.*

Then the Lord said to Moses and Aaron: "Everyone who is 20 years old or more who grumbled against me will not enter the land I swore with uplifted hand to make your home, except Caleb son of Jephunneh and Joshua son of Nun.

For the story of Israel's captivity, please read Exodus 1.

God's Daily Care

Behold, the Lord thy God hath set the land before thee: go up and possess it, as the Lord God of thy fathers hath said to thee, "FEAR NOT, neither be discouraged." Deuteronomy 1:21 (KJV)

For my second surgery, we had to leave our small town and travel to the big city. Number One; Jack doesn't like to drive in big city downtown traffic, and Number Two; I was getting ready to, literally, put my life in the hands of complete strangers.

We found the University Hospital easily—it was just off of the Interstate (how convenient of them to build it so close all those years ago—ha ha!).

But, finding the specialist I needed in that huge facility was a little daunting. When I gave the doctor's name at the Information Desk, they hadn't even heard of him. And, they asked me, why didn't I have the information they needed from the Information Packet that they had sent me (which I didn't receive until I returned home from the hospital)?

Finally, someone at Registration directed us to a station just down the hall. They had never heard of him or me either. I didn't even know what area of medicine he was in.

At last someone on the telephone knew where he was. She gave us vague directions and we set off, already late for my scheduled appointment.

We wandered through halls, past elevators, gift shops and endless stairways. At a juncture of two corridors, Jack pointed to the left, with a shrug, and we took it.

Bursting through a doorway, we saw little flag-like signs attached up near the ceiling and they read; "Inhale," "Exhale," "Inhale," "Exhale," about twenty times. We immediately laughed and our stress was relieved. We thought, at the time, that they were there for just such a situation as ours; lost on the back side of a huge hospital, late for an appointment and all in a dither.

After we got home and cooler heads prevailed, we realized it was probably some measured treatment steps for people with lung problems. Anyway, it did the trick for us.

Deuteronomy 1:21

"Look, the Lord your God has set the land before you; go up and possess it, as the Lord God of your fathers has spoken to you; DO NOT FEAR or be discouraged." (NKJV)

If

If you can keep your head when all about you are losing theirs and blaming it on you;

If you can trust yourself when all men doubt you, but make allowance for their doubting too;

If you can wait and not be tired by waiting, or, being lied about, don't deal in lies,

Or, being hated, don't give way to hating, and yet don't look too good, or talk too wise;

If you can dream—and not make dreams your master;

If you can think—and not make thoughts your aim;

If you can meet with triumph and disaster and treat those two imposters just the same;

If you can bear to hear the truth you've spoken twisted by knaves to make a trap for fools,

Or watch the things you gave your life to broken, and stoop and build 'em up with worn out tools;

If you can make one heap of all your winnings and risk it on one turn of pitch-and-toss,

And lose, and start again at your beginnings and never breathe a word about your loss;

If you can force your heart and nerve and sinew to serve your turn long after they are gone,

And so hold on when there is nothing in you except the will which says to them: "Hold on";

If you can talk with crowds and keep your virtue, or walk with kings—nor lose the common touch;

If neither foes nor loving friends can hurt you;

If all men count with you, but none too much;

If you can fill the unforgiving minute with sixty seconds' worth of distance run—

Yours is the earth and everything that's in it,

And—which is more—you'll be a man, my son!

Joseph Rudyard Kipling (1865-1936) wrote many poems and stories, the most famous being Mowgli's adventures while being raised by animals in *The Jungle Book*. He won the Nobel Prize for Literature in 1907. His own son, John was killed in the Battle of Loos during WWI.

FEAR NOT

#32

SHARING JESUS

"I have learned over the years that when one's mind is made up, this diminishes fear; knowing what must be done does away with fear."

Rosa Parks

Going to War

Deuteronomy 20:1-12 (NKJV)

*When you go out to battle against your enemies, and see horses and chariots and people more numerous than you, **Do not be afraid** of them.*

For the Lord your God is with you, who brought you up from the land of Egypt.

So it shall be, when you are on the verge of battle that the priest shall approach and speak to the people. And he shall say to them, "Hear, O Israel:

"Today you are on the verge of battle with your enemies.

*Do not let your heart faint, **Do not be afraid**, and do not tremble or be terrified because of them.*

For the Lord your God is He who goes with you, to fight for you against your enemies, to save you."

Then the officers shall speak to the people, saying: "What man is there who has built a new house and has not dedicated it?

Let him go and return to his house, lest he dies in the battle and another man dedicates it.

Also what man is there who has planted a vineyard and has not eaten of it?

Let him go and return to his house, lest he dies in the battle and another man eats of it.

And what man is there who is betrothed to a woman and has not married her?

Let him go and return to his house, lest he die in battle and another man marry her."

The officers shall speak further to the people, and say, "What man is there who is fearful and fainthearted? Let him go and return to his house, lest the heart of his brethren faint like his heart."

And so it shall be, when the officers have finished speaking to the people, that they shall make captains of the armies to lead the people.

When you go near a city to fight against it, then proclaim an offer of peace to it.

And it shall be that if they accept your offer of peace, and open to you, then all the people who are found in it shall be placed under tribute to you, and serve you.

Now if the city will not make peace with you, but makes war against you, they you shall besiege it.

For God's covenant with Abraham, please read Genesis 15.

Sharing Jesus

And the priest shall say unto them, "Hear, O Israel, ye approach this day unto battle against your enemies: Let not your hearts faint. FEAR NOT, and do not tremble, neither be ye terrified of them." **Deuteronomy 20:3 (KJV)**

Usually I start out ready to face surgery one day, and then the next day, I'm not ready. Until the very last week before it happens. That week, I am ready every day.

I've thought about how amazing it is that when you face something unpleasant, you can talk with yourself and get prepared for it; with God's help, I mean. I guess I just have to familiarize myself with it. The more I think about it, the easier it gets to deal with.

Now, I know some people are not like this. The more they think about it, the crazier it makes them. Maybe if you're the latter way, this won't help you at all.

But, I do know one thing. If your doctor tells you that a procedure will be a "little uncomfortable," it will be nasty. Remember my prayer time in the bathroom? Sometimes we feel like fainting. Sometimes we feel like trembling. Sometimes we are terrified.

But, don't forget, God is always there.

How do people without Him survive difficult situations? I do not know.

All I know is; I am so thankful that even if I have to travel far away from my home for surgery, or say goodbye to my brother and his family, who are missionaries on the other side of the world, God is always there.

I think the two most exciting things are seeing Jesus in others and introducing others to Jesus. How many times have we said, "I don't know if they're saved or not." That is so sad. How can we share if we don't know? I can't give you an exact guideline for every situation, but if you ask God to help you and you are fully open to His leading, He will. Let's get out there and help Jesus touch the world.

Deuteronomy 20:3

And he shall say to them, "Hear, O Israel: Today you are on the verge of battle with your enemies. Do not let your heart faint, DO NOT BE AFRAID, and do not tremble or be terrified because of them." **(NKJV)**

What a Friend We Have in Jesus

What a friend we have in Jesus, all our sins and griefs to bear.
What a privilege to carry everything to God in prayer.
O what peace we often forfeit, O what needless pain we bear,
All because we do not carry everything to God in prayer.

Have we trials and temptations? Is there trouble anywhere?
We should never be discouraged, take it to the Lord in prayer.
Can we find a friend so faithful who will all our sorrows share?
Jesus knows our every weakness, take it to the Lord in prayer.

Are we weak and heavy-laden, cumbered with a load of care?
Precious Savior, still our refuge—take it to the Lord in prayer.
Do thy friends despise, forsake thee? Take it to the Lord in prayer;
In His arms He'll take and shield thee, thou wilt find a solace there.

Blessed Savior, Thou hast promised Thou wilt all our burdens bear
May we ever, Lord, be bringing all to Thee in earnest prayer.
Soon in glory bright unclouded there will be no need for prayer,
Rapture, praise and endless worship will be our sweet portion there.

Joseph Medlicott Scriven (1819-1886) was born in Ireland and attended Trinity College. The night before he was to be married, his fiancée drowned. Heartbroken, he immigrated to Canada. There he met another, but she died of pneumonia. From then on, he devoted his life to others. This hymn was written to comfort his gravely ill mother.

FEAR NOT

#31

A PLACE TO STAY

"Train yourself to let go of the things you fear to lose."

George Lucas

Life and Death

Deuteronomy 30:11-20 (NKJV)

Deuteronomy 31:1-6 (NKJV)

For this commandment which I command you today is not too mysterious for you, nor is it far off. It is not in heaven, that you should say, "Who will ascend into heaven for us and bring it to us, that we may hear it and do it?" Nor is it beyond the sea, that you should say, "Who will go over the sea for us and bring it to us, that we may hear it and do it?" But the word is very near you, in your mouth and in your heart, that you may do it.

See, I have set before you today life and good, death and evil, in that I command you today to love the Lord your God, to walk in his ways, and to keep his commandments, his statutes, and his judgments, that you may live and multiply; and the Lord your God will bless you in the land which you go to possess.

But if your heart turns away so that you do not hear, and are drawn away, and worship other gods and serve them, I announce to you today that you shall surely perish; you shall not prolong your days in the land which you cross over the Jordan to go in and possess.

I call heaven and earth as witnesses today against you, that I have set before you life and death, blessing and cursing; therefore choose life, that both you and your descendants may live; that you may love the Lord your God, that you may obey His voice, and that you may cling to Him, for He is your life and the length of your days; and that you may dwell in the land which the Lord swore to your fathers, to Abraham, Isaac, and Jacob, to give them.

Then Moses went and spoke these words to all Israel. And he said to them: "I am one hundred and twenty years old today. I can no longer go out and come in. Also the Lord has said to me, 'You shall not cross over this Jordan.' The Lord your God Himself crosses over before you; He will destroy these nations from before you, and you shall dispossess them. Joshua himself crosses over before you, just as the Lord has said.

*"And the Lord will do to them as He did to Sihon and Og, the kings of the Amorites and their land, when He destroyed them. The Lord will give them over to you, that you may do to them according to every commandment which I have commanded you. Be strong and of good courage, **do not fear** or be afraid of them; for the Lord your God, he is the One who goes with you. He will not leave you nor forsake you."*

For the story of Moses' birth and rise to leadership, please read Exodus 2-4.

A Place to Stay

And Moses said, "Be strong and of a good courage, FEAR NOT, nor be afraid of them: for the Lord thy God, He it is that doth go with thee; He will not fail thee, nor forsake thee." Deuteronomy 31:6 (KJV)

Our Pastor recently reminded us to note down and share financial miracles that the Lord has brought our way. I already keep a monthly "Thank You" page in my journal for good (and bad) things that happen. But, after this, I started a page just for financial miracles.

I immediately came up with several that I hadn't even thought about before.

Planning to stay in the big city (Seattle) for my second surgery, we felt truly blessed to find two nearby hotels that offered discount rates to patients.

After this lovely news, my sister-in-law mentioned that they often let a spouse stay in the hospital room if you can prove financial hardship. And, I decided that since I wouldn't be feeling well, Jack could share meals with me as well.

Then, on the very day that I started my financial "Thank You" list, my mother called to say that my stepbrother and his wife had invited us to stay with them while we were there.

I had to go one day early and stay in town a few days after my release because our home is an hour away from any hospital in case of complications.

Now Jack would have the freedom to stay with me if I had a bad day without paying for a reservation that he wouldn't be using.

As our church secretary always says: ***"Isn't God good?"***

You know, He knows all of our needs and even if you have to face a large medical bill, many hospitals will let you pay a percentage based on your income and some doctors even write-off what you owe them.

I know, because these came straight from someone else's financial "Thank You" list.

Deuteronomy 31:6

Moses said, "Be strong and of good courage, DO NOT FEAR nor be afraid of them; for the Lord your God, he is the one who goes with you. He will not leave you nor forsake you." (NKJV)

Drop a Pebble in the Water

Drop a pebble in the water: just a splash, and it is gone;
But there's half-a-hundred ripples circling on and on and on,
Spreading, spreading from the center, flowing on out to the sea.
And there is no way of telling where the end is going to be.

Drop a pebble in the water: in a minute you forget,
But there's little waves a-flowing, and there's ripples circling yet,
And those little waves a-flowing to a great big wave have grown;
You've disturbed a mighty river just by dropping in a stone.

Drop an unkind word, or careless: in a minute it is gone;
But there's half-a-hundred ripples circling on and on and on.
They keep spreading, spreading, spreading from the center as they go.
And there is no way to stop them, once you've started them to flow.

Drop an unkind word, or careless: in a minute you forget;
But there's little waves a-flowing, and there's ripples circling yet,
And perhaps in some sad heart a mighty wave of tears you've stirred,
And disturbed a life was happy ere you dropped that unkind word.

Drop a word of cheer and kindness: just a flash and it is gone;
But there's half-a-hundred ripples circling on and on and on,
Bearing hope and joy and comfort on each splashing, dashing wave
Till you wouldn't believe the volume of the one kind word you gave.

Drop a word of cheer and kindness: in a minute you forget;
But there's gladness still a-swelling, and there's joy a-circling yet.
And you've rolled a wave of comfort whose sweet music can be heard
Over miles and miles of water just by dropping one kind word.

James W. Foley

FEAR NOT

#30

SAFE IN HIS ARMS

"Now all has been heard; here is the conclusion of the matter:

Fear God and keep His commandments, for this is the whole duty of man." **Ecclesiastes 12:13**

King Solomon

Joshua & Moses

Deuteronomy 31:7-13 (NKJV)

Deuteronomy 34:1-5 (NKJV)

Then Moses called Joshua and said to him in the sight of all Israel,

"Be strong and of good courage, for you must go with this people to the land which the Lord has sworn to their fathers to give them, and you shall cause them to inherit it.

"And the Lord, He is the One who goes before you. He will be with you, He will not leave you nor forsake you. **Do not fear** *nor be dismayed."*

So Moses wrote this law and delivered it to the priests, the sons of Levi, who bore the ark of the covenant of the Lord, and to all the elders of Israel.

And Moses commanded them, saying:

"At the end of every seven years, at the appointed time in the year of release, at the Feast of Tabernacles, when all Israel comes to appear before the Lord your God in the place which He chooses, you shall read this law before all Israel in their hearing.

"Gather the people together, men and women and little ones, and the stranger who is within your gates, that they may hear and that they may learn to fear the Lord your God and carefully observe all the words of this law, and that their children, who have not known it, may hear and learn to fear the Lord your God as long as you live in the land which you cross the Jordan to possess."

Then Moses went up from the plains of Moab to Mount Nebo, to the top of Pisgah, which is across from Jericho.

And the Lord showed him all the land of Gilead as far as Dan, all Naphtali and the land of Ephraim and Manasseh, all the land of Judah as far as the Western Sea, the South, and the plain of the Valley of Jericho, the city of palm trees, as far as Zoar.

Then the Lord said to him, "This is the land of which I swore to give Abraham, Isaac, and Jacob, saying, 'I will give it to your descendants.' I have caused you to see it with your eyes, but you shall not cross over there."

So Moses the servant of the Lord died there in the land of Moab, according to the word of the Lord.

For the Song of Moses, please read Deuteronomy 32.

Safe in His Arms

And Moses said, "And the Lord, He it is that doth go before thee; He will be with thee, He will not fail thee, neither forsake thee: FEAR NOT, neither be dismayed." Deuteronomy 31:8 (KJV)

This really spoke to my heart about not being afraid when we go through something we've never gone through before. God says the exact same thing only two verses apart! The children of Israel must have really been scared. And they had forty years for this moment. In this book, I've only give you thirty seven days.

But God has been with you this first week, hasn't He? I can *guarantee* that He will be with you all of the rest, too. Guess what? He was with you before that and He will be with you all the rest of your days. Just like the poem about the "Footprints in the Sand"—when there is only one pair of steps, it is because He is carrying you.

You are never alone and all you have to do is call out to Him.

I have a friend who was in the delivery room with her daughter each of the three times that she gave birth. I asked her how she, as a mother, could stand to see her daughter in so much pain.

She told me she couldn't have done it alone, she just had to pray the entire time for God's strength.

And she was able to stay because He carried her.

I like to think of my time under anesthesia as not lying on the operating table, but resting safely in the arms of Jesus. I know the medical reasons for not being aware of anything around you during that time, but spiritually we are not aware because Jesus has taken us up. If we trust in Him. And how can we not do that? Our weak, little body definitely has its limits, both mentally and physically.

When we get to that point and have no more of us, He will give us all of Him.

I'm a worrier and ashamed of it. If we would get up first thing every day and give it all to Him, we could stop. Let's try it today.

Deuteronomy 31:8

Moses said, "And the Lord, he is the one who goes before you. He will be with you, he will not leave you nor forsake you; DO NOT FEAR nor be dismayed." (NKJV)

Footprints in the Sand

One night a man dreamed he was walking along the beach with the Lord.

As scenes of his life flashed before him, he noticed that there were two sets of footprints in the sand.

He also noticed at his saddest, lowest times there was but one set of footprints.

This bothered the man and he asked the Lord,

"Did you not promise that if I gave my heart to You that You'd be with me all the way?

Then why is there but one set of footprints during my most troublesome times?"

The Lord replied,

"My precious child, I love you and I would never forsake you.

During those times of trial and suffering,

When you see only one set of footprints,

It was then that I carried you."

Margaret Fishback Powers is generally credited with writing this prose poem, but several people claim authorship. Due to heavy marketing, it's too bad that none can legally claim it. I wonder who the money goes to? But disregarding all of that, the first time I read this poem, tears came to my eyes and I was greatly moved. My son and daughter-in-law gave me a picture of the beach with two sets of footprints disappearing into the distance and I greatly cherish it.

FEAR NOT

#29

DO UNTO OTHERS

"The fear of death is more to be dreaded than death itself."

Publilius Syrus

Battle at Ai

Joshua 8:1-23 (NIV)

*Then the Lord said to Joshua, "**Do not be afraid**; do not be discouraged. Take the whole army with you, and go up and attack Ai. For I have delivered into your hands the king of Ai, his people, his city and his land. You shall do to Ai and its king as you did to Jericho and its king, except that you may carry off their plunder and livestock for yourselves. Set an ambush behind the city."*

So Joshua and the whole army moved out to attack Ai. He chose 30,000 of his best fighting men and sent them out at night with these orders: "Listen carefully. You are to set an ambush behind the city. Don't go very far from it. All of you be on the alert. I and all those with me will advance on the city, and when the men come out against us, as they did before, we will flee from them.

"They will pursue us until we have lured them away from the city, for they will say, 'They are running away from us as they did before.' So when we flee from them, you are to rise up from ambush and take the city. The Lord your God will give it into your hand. When you have taken the city, set it on fire. Do what the Lord has commanded. See to it; you have my orders."

Then Joshua sent them off, and they went to the place of ambush and lay in wait.

Early the next morning Joshua mustered his men, and he and the leaders of Israel marched before them to Ai. The entire force that was with him marched up and approached the city and arrived in front of it. They set up camp north of Ai, with the valley between them and the city. Joshua had taken about 5,000 men and set them in ambush to the west of the city. They had the soldiers take up their positions—all those in the camp to the north of the city and the ambush to the west of it.

When the king of Ai saw this, he and all the men of the city hurried out early in the morning to meet Israel in battle at a certain place overlooking the Arabah. But he did not know that an ambush had been set against him behind the city. Joshua and all Israel let themselves be driven back before them, and they fled toward the desert.

All the men of Ai were called to pursue them. Not a man remained in Ai. The men in the ambush rose quickly from their position and rushed forward. They entered the city and captured it and quickly set it on fire. The men of Ai looked back and saw the smoke of the city rising against the sky, but they had no chance to escape in any direction, for the Israelites who had been fleeing toward the desert had turned back against them, so that they were caught in the middle.

For the previous failed battle against Ai, please read Joshua 7.

Do Unto Others

And the Lord said unto Joshua, "FEAR NOT, neither be thou dismayed: take all the people of war with thee, and arise, go up to Ai: see, I have given into thy hand the King of Ai, and his people, and his city, and his land." Joshua 8:1 (KJV)

My second surgery was a lot more delicate than the first one with the possibility of more severe complications. One day, pre-surgery, I began to dwell on those "what-ifs" and pretty well had myself convinced that I wasn't going to survive the surgery.

In fact, that day is today and here is how I feel as I'm writing this.

My first thought, after Heaven, is, what do I need to do to prepare?

Before I go in for surgery, I always pay all of the bills, clean the entire house, wash everyone's clothes, and bake a cake. This time I also wrote thank you notes, just this morning, not mentioning my fear, but thanking family and friends for the little things that they do. But what about Jack and our two kids, Laurie and Delano?

Way down in the bottom of the bill drawer, I wrote their names on the outside of a piece of my favorite stationery and circled them. On the inside I wrote: "I love you and you know where I am. Grandpa and I will be waiting for you there. Love, Mom. (Bye-bye, Sweetie)."

Jesus could come at any time and our Pastor is always suggesting that we live each day as if it were our last.

What about a phone call or a visit to the sick and elderly? Who could use a fresh-baked cake?

What about *"a soft answer turneth away wrath"* (Proverbs 15:1 KJV)? Just like the song, "To Be Like Jesus," that's all I ask.

What if this was your last day on earth? What would you do?

There now, I feel better about that, don't you?

Joshua 8:1

Now the Lord said to Joshua: "DO NOT BE AFRAID, nor dismayed; take all the people of war with you, and arise, go up to Ai. See, I have given into your hand the king of Ai, his people, his city, and his land." (NKJV)

A Soul's Soliloquy

Today the journey is ended,
I have worked out the mandates of fate;
Naked, alone, undefended,
I knock at the Uttermost Gate.

Behind is life and its longing,
Its trial, its trouble, its sorrow;
Beyond is the Infinite Morning
Of a day without a tomorrow.

Go back to dust and decay,
Body, grown weary and old;
You are worthless to me from today—
No longer my soul can you hold.

I lay you down gladly forever
For a life that is better than this;
I go where partings ne'er sever
You into oblivion's abyss.

Lo, the gate swings wide at my knocking,
Across endless reaches I see
Lost friends with laughter come flocking
To give a glad welcome to me.

Farewell, the maze has been threaded,
This is the ending of strife;
Say not that death should be dreaded—
'Tis but the beginning of life.

Wenonah Stevens Abbott (1865-1950) was an American journalist, writer and lecturer.

FEAR NOT

#28

SATAN IS THE LOSER

"Fear does not have any special power unless you empower it by submitting to it."

Les Brown

Five Amorite Kings

Joshua 10:5-25 (NKJV)

Therefore the five kings of the Amorites gathered together and went up, they and all their armies, and camped before Gibeon and made war against it. And the men of Gibeon sent to Joshua at the camp at Gilgal, saying, "Do not forsake your servants; come up to us quickly, save us and help us, for all the kings of the Amorites who dwell in the mountains have gathered together against us."

*So Joshua ascended from Gilgal, he and all the people of war with him, and all the mighty men of valor. And the Lord said to Joshua, "**Do not fear** them, for I have delivered them into your hand; not a man of them shall stand before you." Joshua therefore came upon them suddenly, having marched all night from Gilgal. So the Lord routed them before Israel.*

Then Joshua spoke to the Lord in the day when the Lord delivered up the Amorites before the children of Israel, and he said in the sight of Israel:

"Sun, stand still over Gibeon; and Moon, in the Valley of Aijalon."

So the sun stood still, and the moon stopped, till the people had revenge upon their enemies. Is this not written in the Book of Jasher? So the sun stood still in the midst of heaven, and did not hasten to go down for about a whole day. And there has been no day like that, before it or after it, that the Lord heeded the voice of a man; for the Lord fought for Israel.

But these five kings had fled and hidden themselves in a cave at Makkedah. So Joshua said, "Roll large stones against the mouth of the cave, and set men by it to guard them."

Then it happened, while Joshua and the children of Israel made an end of slaying them with a very great slaughter, till they had finished, that those who escaped entered fortified cities.

Then Joshua said, "Open the mouth of the cave, and bring those five kings to me from the cave." And they did so, and brought out those five kings to him from the cave.

Joshua called for all the men of Israel, and said to the captains of the men of war who went with him, "Come near, put your feet on the necks of these kings." And they drew near and put their feet on their necks.

*Then Joshua said to them, "**Do not be afraid**, nor be dismayed; be strong and of good courage, for thus the Lord will do to all your enemies against whom you fight."*

For the story of Aaron and Hur holding up Moses' hands during battle, please read Exodus 17.

Satan is the Loser

And Joshua said unto them, "FEAR NOT, nor be dismayed, be strong and of good courage: for thus shall the Lord do to all your enemies against whom ye fight." Joshua 10:25 (KJV)

Every day, when I ask the Lord to help me know what to share for this devotional, I panic a little and wonder what would happen if I couldn't think of anything to write.

That's just another fear, isn't it?

Sometimes thoughts come to me when I'm washing the dishes, crocheting a baby afghan, or driving to town.

One of our retired lay ministers once shared that God speaks most often to our hearts during our daily devotions. I completely agree.

This may sound a little bit corny, but the verse that stood out to me today was the one about the necks of the five kings (verse 24). Not because of any submission/dominance symbolism, but because I was actually having surgery on my neck.

Hey, remember, everything in the Bible can be applied to our daily lives and this sure did, to mine, at this very moment.

But, the more I think about it, it also shows our authority over Satan. I will probably never fight against five kings, but I fight against Satan every day.

The Bible says he is the loser and that *he can never win.*

So, whatever you're struggling with today can be overcome with God's help. That's a promise from me, and, more importantly, from God.

Postscript: Did you know that computers have recently discovered that "somehow" in our past, a day was actually "lost" from the reckoning of man? Computers proving the truth of the Bible, praise God!

Joshua 10:25

Then Joshua said to them, "DO NOT BE AFRAID, nor be dismayed; be strong and of good courage, for thus the Lord will do to all your enemies against whom you fight." (NKJV)

Where There's a Will There's a Way

We have faith in old proverbs full surely, for wisdom has traced what they tell,

And truth may be drawn up as purely from them, as it may from "a well."

Let us question the thinkers and doers, and hear what they honestly say;

And you'll find they believe, like bold wooers, in "where there's a will there's a way."

The hills have been high for man's mounting, the woods have been dense for his axe,

The stars have been thick for his counting, the sands have been wide for his tracks,

The sea has been deep for his diving, the poles have been broad for his sway,

But bravely he's proved in his striving, that "where there's a will there's a way."

Have ye vices that ask a destroyer? Or passions that need your control?

Let reason become your employer, and your body be ruled by your soul.

Fight on, though ye bleed in the trial, resist with all strength that ye may;

Ye may conquer sin's host by denial, for "where there's a will there's a way."

Have ye poverty's pinching to cope with? Does suffering weigh down your might?

Only call up a spirit to hope with, and dawn may come out of the night.

Oh! Much may be done by defying the ghosts of despair and dismay;

And much may be gained by relying on "where there's a will there's a way."

Should ye see afar off that worth winning, set out on the journey with trust;

And ne'er heed if your path at beginning should be among brambles and dust.

Though it is but by footsteps ye do it, and hardships may hinder and stay,

Walk with faith, and be sure you'll get through it; for "where there's a will there's a way."

Eliza Cook (1818-1889) was a writer and poet from England who was encouraged by her church's music master to publish her first book of poetry at the age of 17. She went on to write articles and poems for national magazines, the most well-known being *The Fair Rose of Killarney*.

FEAR NOT

#27

WHY ME, LORD?

"In God, whose word I praise, in God I trust; I will not be afraid.

What can mortal man do to me?" Psalm 56:4

King David

Gideon & Midian

Judges 6:10-23 (NIV)

Again the Israelites did evil in the eyes of the Lord, and for seven years he gave them into the hands of the Midianites. Because the power of Midian was so oppressive, the Israelites prepared shelters for themselves in mountain clefts, caves and strongholds. Whenever the Israelites planted their crops, the Midianites invaded the country. They camped on the land and ruined the crops all the way to Gaza and did not spare a living thing for Israel, neither sheep nor cattle nor donkeys. They came up with their livestock and their tents like swarms of locusts.

When the Israelites cried to the Lord because of Midian, he sent them a prophet, who said, "This is what the Lord, the God of Israel, says: I brought you up out of Egypt, out of the land of slavery. I snatched you from the power of Egypt and from the hand of all your oppressors. I drove them from before you and gave you their land. I said to you, 'I am the Lord your God. **Do not be afraid** *of the gods of the Amorites, in whose land you live.' But you have not listened to me."*

The angel of the Lord came and sat down under the oak in Ophrah that belonged to Joash the Abiezrite, where his son Gideon was threshing wheat in a winepress to keep it from the Midianites. When the angel of the Lord appeared to Gideon, he said, "The Lord is with you, mighty warrior."

"But sir," Gideon replied, "if the Lord is with us, why has all this happened to us? Where are all his wonders that our fathers told us about when they said, 'Did not the Lord bring us up out of Egypt?' But now the Lord has abandoned us and put us into the hand of Midian."

The Lord turned to him and said, "Go in the strength you have and save Israel out of Midian's hand." "But Lord," Gideon asked, "how can I save Israel? My clan is the weakest in Manasseh, and I am the least in my family." The Lord answered, "I will be with you, and you will strike down all the Midianites together."

Gideon replied, "If now I have found favor in your eyes, give me a sign that it is really you talking to me." Gideon went in, prepared a young goat, and from an ephah of flour he made bread without yeast. Putting the meat in a basket and its broth in a pot, he brought them out and offered them to him under the oak.

The angel of God said to him, "Take the meat and the unleavened bread, place them on this rock, and pour out the broth." And Gideon did so. With the tip of the staff that was in his hand, the angel of the Lord touched the meat and the unleavened bread. Fire flared from the rock, consuming the meat and the bread. And the angel of the Lord disappeared.

For the rest of Gideon's life story, please read Judges 8.

Why Me, Lord?

And I said unto you, "I am the Lord your God; FEAR NOT the gods of the Amorites, in whose land ye dwell: but ye have not obeyed my voice." Judges 6:10 (KJV)

There was Gideon, minding his own business, quietly threshing wheat in a secret hiding place so that the Midianites wouldn't take it away from him and eat it all up. Just minding his own business and an angel of the Lord comes down to tell him that he has a hard job to do.

But he is to do it for God and God will help him.

Have you ever felt that your illness or pain or stress or grief wasn't fair? I have, of course, but let's try not to think of it that way. Think of it as doing something for God; or going through something with God, and all for His glory.

If we never had to struggle, we couldn't understand, or empathize with the struggles of others. If God always spared us, we wouldn't be where we are today in our Christian walk.

Imagine Gideon frantically trying to prove that this was an angel and that it really was God's will. Later on he gets down to asking for dry and wet fleeces.

Am I like that?

I have found that we don't even have to ask for signs. God simply opens or closes doors. Whatever situation you are in (even if you made a sinful choice) you are there for a reason.

Always, always to show God's glory or His forgiveness.

Those tough times are when we can be the strongest witness. It's when everything is bad and you are still in control (with God's help), that people begin to wonder how you do it. And maybe they'll start to ask questions.

And maybe somewhere a door or a heart will open.

And maybe somewhere an angel will rejoice.

Judges 6:10

Also I said to you, "I am the Lord your God; DO NOT FEAR the gods of the Amorites, in whose land you dwell." But you have not obeyed my voice. (NKJV)

Try Smiling

When the weather suits you not,

Try smiling.

When your coffee isn't hot,

Try smiling.

When your neighbors don't do right,

Or your relatives all fight,

Sure 'tis hard, but then you might

Try smiling.

Doesn't change the things, of course—

Just smiling.

But it cannot make them worse—

Just smiling.

And it seems to help your case,

Brightens up a gloomy place,

Then, it sort o' rests your face—

Just smiling.

Author Unknown

FEAR NOT

#26

LORD IS PEACE

"There are only two ways to live your life. One is as though nothing is a miracle.

The other is as though everything is a miracle."

Albert Einstein

Gideon's Fleece

Judges 6:22-40 (NKJV)

Now Gideon perceived that he was the angel of the Lord. So Gideon said, "Alas, O Lord God! For I have seen the angel of the Lord face to face." Then the Lord said to him, "Peace be with you; **Do not fear***, you shall not die."*

So Gideon built an altar there to the Lord, and called it The-Lord-Is-Peace. To this day it is still in Ophrah of the Abiezrites. Now it came to pass the same night that the Lord said to him, "Take your father's young bull, the second bull of seven years old, and tear down the altar of Baal that your father has, and cut down the wooden image that is beside it; and build an altar to the Lord your God on top of this rock in the proper arrangement, and take the second bull and offer a burnt sacrifice with the wood of the image which you shall cut down."

So Gideon took ten men from among his servants and did as the Lord had said to him. But because he feared his father's household and the men of the city too much to do it by day, he did it by night. And when the men of the city arose early in the morning, there was the altar of Baal, torn down; and the wooden image that was beside it was cut down, and the second bull was being offered on the altar which had been built.

So they said to one another, "Who has done this thing?" And when they had inquired and asked, they said, "Gideon the son of Joash has done this thing." Then the men of the city said to Joash, "Bring out your son, that he may die, because he has torn down the altar of Baal, and because he has cut down the wooden image that was beside it." But Joash said to all who stood against him, "Would you plead for Baal? Would you save him? Let the one who would plead for him be put to death by morning! If he is a god, let him plead for himself, because his altar has been torn down!"

Then all the Midianites gathered together; and they crossed over and encamped in the Valley of Jezreel. But the Spirit of the Lord came upon Gideon; then he blew the trumpet and the Abiezrites gathered behind him.

So Gideon said to God, "If You will save Israel by my hand as You have said—look, I shall put a fleece of wool on the threshing floor; if there is dew on the fleece only, and it is dry on all the ground, then I shall know that You will save Israel by my hand, as You have said." And it was so.

Then Gideon said to God, "Do not be angry with me, but let me speak just once more: Let me test, I pray, just once more with the fleece; let it now be dry only on the fleece, but on all the ground let there be dew." And God did so that night. It was dry on the fleece only, but there was dew on all the ground.

For Gideon's defeat of the great Midianite army, please read Judges 7.

The Lord is Peace

And the Lord said unto Gideon, "Peace be unto thee; FEAR NOT: thou shalt not die." Judges 6:23 (KJV)

Have you ever been asked to bring a living will with you on the day of your surgery? That is a little scary.

I remember the day I called our lawyer's secretary to get the paperwork started and she wanted to know what my surgery was for.

She said things like, "Oh, no, that's bad," or "Oh, my, I hope you're going to be alright."

Then she asked me how I was feeling about it and I thought to myself that I was feeling pretty good until I talked to her!

In the midst of thinking about my own mortality, both of our kids missed being involved in car accidents by just minutes.

In Laurie's case, she forgot to gas her car up the day before, so as she was doing this the next day, a friend drove by and waved.

On her way home, that same friend was directing traffic around a very bad wreck.

Two days later, Delano decided to do just one more chore before he left town. On the way home, he was detoured around another wreck where a car had lost control and sheared-off a power pole.

If he hadn't done that one last chore, he would have been heading out of town at the exact same time the future accident was heading in.

And there was a fatality in that last wreck.

Now, believe it or not, I didn't even look at today's verse or read the chapter before I started to write this. It says, ***"Thou shalt not die."*** I could take this to mean that I will survive this surgery, or, as in Gideon's case, that he would survive the battle.

But I also like to think of it in terms of eternity. In Heaven we never have to fear death anymore.

Judges 6:23

Then the Lord said to him, "Peace be with you; DO NOT FEAR, you shall not die." (NKJV)

It is Well With My Soul

When peace like a river, attendeth my way, when sorrows like sea billows roll;

Whatever my lot, Thou hast taught me to say, "It is well, it is well with my soul."

Though Satan should buffet, though trials should come, let this blest assurance control;

That Christ has regarded my helpless estate, and hath shed His own blood for my soul.

My sin—oh, the bliss of this glorious thought—my sin—not in part, but the whole,

Is nailed to the cross and I bear it no more, praise the Lord, praise the Lord, O my soul!

For me, be it Christ, be it Christ hence to live: If Jordan above me shall roll,

No pang shall be mine, for in death as in life Thou wilt whisper Thy peace to my soul.

But, Lord, 'tis for Thee, for Thy coming we wait, the sky, not the grave, is our goal;

Oh trump of the angel! Oh voice of the Lord! Blessed hope, blessed rest of my soul!

And, Lord, haste the day when the faith shall be sight, the clouds be rolled back as a scroll,

The trump shall resound and the Lord shall descend, "Even so, it is well with my soul."

It is well, it is well.

With my soul, with my soul.

It is well, it is well with my soul.

Horatio G. Spafford (1828-1888) wrote this song as he crossed the Atlantic Ocean to join his wife in Europe. When his ship was at a certain point, the words to this song poured into his soul. The spot he sought was the resting place of his four daughters who had drowned when their ship was hit and sunk just a few weeks before. Only his wife had survived the terrible tragedy. Knowing that his girls were Christians, he knew he would meet them again in Heaven, and God gave him peace. God also gave he and his wife three more children (just like Job).

FEAR NOT

#25

I CHOOSE JOY

"Tis foolish to fear what you cannot avoid."

Publilius Syrus

Fall of Jerusalem

2 Kings 25:1-24 (NKJV)

Now it came to pass in the ninth year of his reign, that Nebuchadnezzar king of Babylon and all his army came against Jerusalem and encamped against it; and they built a siege wall against it all around. So the city was besieged until the eleventh year of King Zedekiah. By the ninth day of the fourth month the famine had become so severe in the city that there was no food for the people of the land. Then the city wall was broken through, and all the men of war fled at night by way of the gate between two walls.

But the army of the Chaldeans pursued the king, and they overtook him in the plains of Jericho. All his army was scattered from him. So they took the king and brought him up to the king of Babylon at Riblah, and they pronounced judgment on him and took him to Babylon.

Nebuzaradan the captain of the guard, a servant of the king of Babylon, came to Jerusalem. He burned the house of the Lord and the king's house and all the houses of Jerusalem. And all the army of the Chaldeans who were with the captain of the guard broke down the walls of Jerusalem all around. Then Nebuzaradan the captain of the guard carried away captive the rest of the people who remained in the city and the defectors who had deserted to the king of Babylon, with the rest of the multitude. But the captain of the guard left some of the poor of the land as vinedressers and farmers.

The bronze pillars that were in the house of the Lord, and the carts and bronze Sea that were in the house of the Lord, the Chaldeans broke in pieces, and carried the bronze to Babylon. They also took away the pots, the shovels, the trimmers, the spoons, and all the bronze utensils with which the priests ministered.

And the captain of the guard took Seraiah the chief priest, Zephaniah the second priest, and the three doorkeepers. He also took out of the city an officer who had charge of the men of war, five men of the king's close associates who were found in the city, the chief recruiting officer of the army, who mustered the people of the land, and sixty men of the people of the land who were found in the city.

Thus Judah was carried away captive from its own land. Then he made Gedaliah the son of Ahikam, the son of Shaphan, governor over the people who remained in the land of Judah, whom Nebuchadnezzar king of Babylon had left. And Gedaliah took an oath before them and their men, and said to them, **"Do not be afraid** *of the servants of the Chaldeans. Dwell in the land and serve the king of Babylon, and it shall be well with you."*

For the story of Israel rebuilding the walls of Jerusalem, please read Nehemiah 2-6.

I Choose Joy

And Gedaliah swore to them, and to their men, and said unto them, "FEAR NOT to be the servants of the Chaldees: dwell in the land, and serve the King of Babylon; and it shall be well with you." **2 Kings 25:24 (KJV)**

What would it be like to have your country overrun and be taken away by an invading force? No longer in charge of your government. No longer in charge of your own life. This has happened in many countries around the world. But not here. Not to us. Not yet.

Three months after my second surgery and eleven months after my first surgery, I was attacked by an invading force—cancer. I know, you're probably thinking what else can happen to this woman? I'll admit, I've asked that myself many times, and I was very, very scared.

But guess what? God was still with me. Even if I have to dwell with this strange ruler in charge of my tissue, God is still in charge over that.

African and Asian people suffering under cruel leaders have the most peace with God that I've ever seen. That's because everything around them is out of control and the only stable thing is God. They become so close to God because nothing else matters. Maybe that is what adversity is all about—drawing us closer to God.

Adversity makes us realize that nothing lasts; not our jobs, not this world, not our bodies.

I know, that if my cancer advances, God will be with me just like He was with me through my surgeries. If you thought I faced death before, you can't imagine what this is like; unless you've been there.

I recently read about someone with a fatal, painful and debilitating disease who said, "Only those people prepared to die are really prepared to live."

No matter what happens, no matter where God takes me with this, I choose joy. We can't base our attitude on what's going on in or around us; it has to be based on God's love for us.

And that love never changes.

2 Kings 25:24

And Gedaliah took an oath before them and their men, and said to them, DO NOT BE AFRAID of the servants of the Chaldeans. Dwell in the land and serve the king of Babylon, and it shall be well with you." **(NKJV)**

Happiness

Happiness is like a crystal, fair and exquisite and clear,

Broken in a million pieces, shattered, scattered far and near.

Now and then along life's pathway, Lo! Some shining fragments fall;

But there are so many pieces

No one ever finds them all.

You may find a bit of beauty, or an honest share of wealth,

While another just beside you gathers honor, love or health.

Vain to choose or grasp unduly, broken is the perfect ball;

And there are so many pieces

No one ever finds them all.

Yet the wise as on their journey treasure every fragment clear,

Fit them as they may together, imaging the shattered sphere,

Learning ever to be thankful, though their share of it is small;

For it has so many pieces

No one ever finds them all.

Priscilla Leonard was the pen name of Emily Perkins Bissell (1861-1948) an American social worker best known as the woman who introduced Christmas Seals to the United States. The idea was to buy a special seal for your letters, the proceeds to be used for the fight against tuberculosis. During the first year, she raised over $3,000 for a local sanitarium. The next year, Howard Pyle, a famous illustrator, donated his art for the design of a new stamp.

FEAR NOT

#24

TIME IS PRECIOUS

"The central struggle of parenthood is to let our hopes for our children outweigh our fears."

Ellen Goodman

David & Solomon

1 Chronicles 28:5-21(NKJV)

Then King David rose to his feet and said, "Of all my sons (for the Lord has given me many sons) he has chosen my son Solomon to sit on the throne of the kingdom of the Lord over Israel. As for you, my son Solomon, know the God of your father, and serve Him with a loyal heart and with a willing mind; for the Lord searches all hearts and understands all the intent of the thought. If you seek Him, he will be found by you; but if you forsake Him, He will cast you off forever. Consider now, for the Lord has chosen you to build a house for the sanctuary; be strong, and do it."

Then David gave his son Solomon the plans for the vestibule, its houses, its treasuries, its upper chambers, its inner chambers, and the place of the mercy seat; and the plans for all that he had by the Spirit, of the courts of the house of the Lord, of all the chambers all around, of the treasuries of the house of God, and the treasuries for the dedicated things; also for the division of the priests and the Levites, for all the work of the service of the house of the Lords, and for all the articles of service in the house of the Lord.

He gave gold by weight for things of gold, for all articles used in every kind of service; also silver for all articles of silver by weight, for all articles used in every kind of service; the weight for the lampstands of gold, and their lamps of gold, by weight for each lampstand and its lamps; for the lampstands of silver by weight, for the lampstand and its lamps, according to the use of each lampstand. And by weight he gave gold for the tables of the showbread, for each table, and silver for the tables of silver; also pure gold for the forks, the basins, the pitchers of pure gold, and the golden bowls—he gave gold by weight for every bowl; and for the silver bowls, silver by weight for every bowl; and refined gold by weight for the altar of incense, and for the construction of the chariot, that is, the gold cherubim that spread their wings and overshadowed the ark of the covenant of the Lord.

"All this," said David, "the Lord made me understand in writing, by his hand upon me, all the works of these plans."

And David said to his son Solomon, "Be strong and of good courage, and do it; ***Do not fear*** *nor be dismayed, for the Lord God—my God—will be with you. He will not leave you nor forsake you, until you have finished all the work for the service of the house of the Lord. Here are the divisions of the priests and the Levites for all the service of the house of God; and every willing craftsman will be with you for all manner of workmanship, for every kind of service; also the leaders and all the people will be completely at your command."*

For the story of Solomon building the temple, please read 2 Chronicles 2-6.

Time is Precious

And David said to Solomon his son, "Be strong and of good courage, and do it: FEAR NOT, nor be dismayed: for the Lord God, even my God, will be with thee; He will not fail thee, nor forsake thee, until thou hast finished all the work for the service of the House of the Lord." 1 Chronicles 28:20 (KJV)

"He will not fail me until all of my work is done." What is my work? First of all, I am to be about my Father's business: living a Christian life and sharing that life with others; a wife and helpmeet for my husband (not a nag); a mother that my children will ***"arise up and call blessed"***; a daughter; a friend; a neighbor—and do all to the glory of God and His Gospel.

Every single minute of every single day is important, and you know it! Remember how you felt when you didn't think that you were going to have very many minutes left? What was the first thing that you wanted? More time with your family. So, while we still have that time, let's not waste it.

Sixty years ago, a woman was on her deathbed, but for some reason she just kept hanging on. One day they told her that her first great-grandson had been born and now there was someone to carry on the family name. She passed away that very day.

That great-grandson was my husband, Jack.

Have you ever had friends with a preemie baby, or had one yourself? We know a couple with two boys and both were very tiny at birth, just as their parents were. As you stand over them and see all of those tubes and wires running in and out, what do you pray for? Time to get to know these little ones and see them grow up. Time to share Bible stories with them and watch them pretend to be David, or Noah, or Adam. Time to see their own children and their children's children.

Let's get out there and ***"do the work"*** we need to do regardless of how much time we have. No matter where we are; at home, at work, at church, we can touch people's lives and have an impact, sometimes without even saying a word.

So, what are we waiting for?

1 Chronicles 28:20

And David said to his son Solomon, "Be strong and of good courage, and do it; DO NOT FEAR nor be dismayed, for the Lord God—my God—will be with you. He will not leave you nor forsake you, until you have finished all the work for the service of the house of the Lord." (NKJV)

The Loom of Time

Man's life is laid in the loom of time
To a pattern he does not see,
While the weavers work and the shuttles fly
Till the dawn of eternity.

Some shuttles are filled with silver threads
And some with threads of gold,
While often but the darker hues
Are all that they may hold.

But the Weaver watches with skillful eye
Each shuttle fly to and fro,
And sees the pattern so deftly wrought
As the loom moves sure and slow.

God surely planned the pattern:
Each thread, the dark and fair,
Is chosen by His master skill
And placed in the web with care.

He only knows its beauty,
And guides the shuttles which hold
The threads so unattractive,
As well as the threads of gold.

Not till each loom is silent,
And the shuttles cease to fly,
Shall God reveal the pattern
And explain the reason why.

The dark threads were as needful
In the weaver's skillful hand
As the threads of gold and silver
For the pattern which He planned.

Author Unknown

FEAR NOT

#23

GOD IS ON MY SIDE

"You can discover what your enemy fears most by observing the means he uses to frighten you."

Eric Hoffer

Jehoshaphat & Moab

2 Chronicles 20:1-17 (NIV)

After this, the Moabites and Ammonites came to make war on Jehoshaphat. Some men came and told Jehoshaphat, "A vast army is coming against you from Edom, from the other side of the Dead Sea. It is already in En Gedi." Alarmed, Jehoshaphat resolved to inquire of the Lord, and he proclaimed a fast for all Judah. The people of Judah came together to seek help from the Lord; indeed, they came from every town in Judah to seek him.

Then Jehoshaphat stood up in the assembly of Judah and Jerusalem at the temple of the Lord in front of the new courtyard and said:

"O Lord, God of our fathers, are you not the God who is in heaven? You rule over all the kingdoms of the nations. Power and might are in your hand, and no one can withstand you. O, our God, did you not drive out the inhabitants of this land before your people Israel and give it forever to the descendants of Abraham your friend? They have lived in it and have built in it a sanctuary for your Name, saying, 'If calamity comes upon us, whether the sword of judgment, of plague or famine, we will stand in Your presence before this temple that bears Your Name and will cry out to You in our distress, and You will hear us and save us.'

"But now here are men from Ammon, Moab, and Mount Seir, whose territory you would not allow Israel to invade when they came from Egypt; so they turned away from them and did not destroy them. See how they are repaying us by coming to drive us out of the possession you gave us as an inheritance. O our God, will you not judge them? For we have no power to face this vast army that is attacking us. We do not know what to do, but our eyes are upon You."

All the men of Judah, with their wives and children and little ones, stood there before the Lord.

Then the Spirit of the Lord came upon Jahaziel, a Levite and descendant of Asaph, as he stood in the assembly.

*He said: "Listen, King Jehoshaphat and all who live in Judah and Jerusalem! This is what the Lord says to you: '**Do not be afraid** or discouraged because of this vast army. For the battle is not yours, but God's. Tomorrow march down against them. You will not have to fight this battle. Take up your positions: stand firm and see the deliverance the Lord will give you. O Judah and Jerusalem. **Do not be afraid**; do not be discouraged. Go out to face them tomorrow, and the Lord will be with you.'"*

For the story of the battle against Moab, please read 2 Chronicles 20:20-30.

God is on My Side

Jehoshaphat said, "Ye shall not need to fight in this battle: set yourselves, stand ye still and see the salvation of the Lord with you, O Judah and Jerusalem: FEAR NOT, nor be dismayed; tomorrow go out against them: for the Lord will be with you." 2 Chronicles 20:17 (KJV)

They didn't do anything except cry out to the Lord in fear, fast, receive the Word, worship and praise Him. What a wonderful prescription for fear!

God fought the battle for them. They didn't even have to touch the enemy. The enemy destroyed themselves.

God will fight our battles for us too. All we have to do is cry out to Him and share our humanness with Him. Then we must fast, read the Word, worship and praise Him. And praise Him again.

Before any major surgery, you are forbidden to eat or drink anything. Usually that is a great excuse for complaining.

But think of it as a fast before the Lord.

This is the time to really get right with the Lord; literally and figuratively. And we don't have to worry because the battle (surgery) is in His hands.

He puts the gift in the doctor's hands, He keeps your heart beating when you're under anesthesia, He causes your bones to knit and your body to heal.

And if He chooses for your life to be over, that is a time of great rejoicing in Heaven because a child is coming home.

To be at peace whether you live or die is the goal. Heaven is just a continuation of life; only much more glorious and perfect. Our human minds can't even begin to imagine what it will be like over there.

But what I look forward to most is seeing Jesus. To thank Him for caring about and loving even me. To worship Him and be in His presence for all of eternity. I can't even imagine that, can you?

Will we miss our earthly family and friends? Let's just make sure that they'll be joining us later, okay?

2 Chronicles 20:17

"You will not need to fight in this battle. Position yourselves, stand still and see the salvation of the Lord, who is with you, O Judah and Jerusalem! DO NOT FEAR or be dismayed; tomorrow go out against them, for the Lord is with you." (NKJV)

The Rose Still Grows Beyond the Wall

Near a shady wall a rose once grew,
Budded and blossomed in God's free light,
Watered and fed by morning dew,
Shedding its sweetness day and night.

As it grew and blossomed fair and tall,
Slowly rising to loftier height,
It came to a crevice in the wall,
Through which there shone a beam of light.

Onward it crept with added strength,
With never a thought of fear or pride.
It followed the light through the crevice's length
And unfolded itself on the other side.

The light, the dew, the broadening view
Were found the same as they were before;
And it lost itself in beauties new,
Breathing its fragrance more and more.

Shall claim of death cause us to grieve,
And make our courage faint or fail?
Nay! Let us faith and hope receive:
The rose still grows beyond the wall.

Scattering fragrance far and wide,
Just as it did in days of yore,
Just as it did on the other side,
Just as it will for evermore.

A.L. Frink

FEAR NOT

#22

CRY TO THE LORD

"The only real prison is fear, and the only real freedom is freedom from fear."

Aung San Suu Kyi

Give Thanks

Psalms 118:1-17 (NKJV)

Oh, give thanks to the Lord, for He is good; His mercy endures forever!

Let Israel now say, "His mercy endures forever."

Let the house of Aaron now say, "His mercy endures forever."

Let those who fear the Lord now say, "His mercy endures forever."

I called on the Lord in distress; the Lord answered me and set me in a broad place.

*The Lord is on my side; I will **not be afraid**, what can man do to me?*

The Lord is for me among those who help me; therefore I shall see my desire on those who hate me.

It is better to trust in the Lord than to put confidence in man.

It is better to trust in the Lord than to put confidence in princes.

All nations surrounded me, but in the name of the Lord I will destroy them

They surrounded me, yes, they surrounded me, but in the name of the Lord I will destroy them.

They surrounded me like bees; they were quenched like a fire of thorns.

You pushed me violently, that I might fall, but the Lord helped me.

The Lord is my strength and song, and He has become my salvation.

The voice of rejoicing and salvation is in the tents of the righteous.

The right hand of the Lord is exalted; the right hand of the Lord does valiantly.

I shall not die, but live, and declare the works of the Lord.

For the story of David conquering Jerusalem and the Philistines, please read 2 Samuel 5.

Cry to the Lord

***The Lord is on my side; I will FEAR NOT: what can man do unto me?* Psalm 118:6 (KJV)**

I had to have minor surgery on my hand to remove all vestiges of the melanoma. When I walked into the operating room, the doctor had on scrubs and a long, hard plastic face protector. I think it was the face protector that got to me. It finally sank in that this thing in me was very deadly, and my knees began to knock together.

"In my anguish I cried to the Lord."

When he began to explain the extent of the removal; flesh as well as the meat on the back of my hand, I looked up at my nurse, Whitney, and she smiled.

I said, "My knees are shaking and they won't stop."

I'll never forget what she said. "Just bend your knees and that will help." And it did! Such a simple thing. You probably thought that since I went through all of these frightening experiences and lived to write about it, that I had no fear. If you thought that, you were wrong.

The point is, yes, we're often scared, but guess what? Jesus is *always* there to walk right beside us as we go through it. I'm not kidding. Every time that we call on Him, He is there. Every single time. That's a promise from me and from Him.

We do have to do our part, though. What is that, you may ask?

"Just bend your knees and that will help."

Submit yourself to His will and ask Him for His strength.

He will *always* help us through it.

He will *always* help us do it.

What more can we ask as we travel down this road called life?

"And He answered by setting me free!"

Psalm 118:6

***The Lord is on my side; I WILL NOT FEAR. What can man do to me?* (NKJV)**

This, Too, Shall Pass Away

When some great sorrow, like a mighty river,

Flows through your life with peace-destroying power,

And dearest things are swept from sight forever,

Say to your heart each trying hour: "This, too, shall pass away."

When ceaseless toil has hushed your song of gladness,

And you have grown almost too tired to pray,

Let this truth banish from your heart its sadness,

And ease the burdens of each trying day: "This, too, shall pass away."

When fortune smiles, and, full of mirth and pleasure,

The days are flitting by without a care,

Lest you should rest with only earthly treasure,

Let these few words their fullest import bear: "This, too, shall pass away."

When earnest labor brings you fame and glory,

And all earth's noblest ones upon you smile,

Remember that life's longest, grandest story

Fills but a moment in earth's little while: "This, too, shall pass away."

Lanta Wilson Smith

FEAR NOT

#21

TRUST IN THE LORD

"I have come to realize that all my trouble with living has come from fear and smallness within me."

Angela L. Wozniak

Wisdom

Proverbs 3:13-31 (NKJV)

Happy is the man who finds wisdom, and the man who gains understanding;

For wisdom is better than profits from silver, and gain from fine gold.

Wisdom is more precious than rubies, and the things you may desire cannot compare with her.

Length of days is in wisdom's right hand, in her left hand riches and honor.

Wisdom's ways are ways of pleasantness, and all her paths are peace.

Wisdom is a tree of life to those who take hold of her, and happy are all who retain her.

The Lord by wisdom founded the earth; by understanding he established the heavens.

By his knowledge the depths were broken up, and clouds drop down the dew.

My son, let them not depart from your eyes—keep sound wisdom and discretion;

So they will be life to your soul and grace to your neck.

Then you will walk safely in your way, and your foot will not stumble.

When you lie down, you will not be afraid;

Yes, you will lie down and your sleep will be sweet.

Do not be afraid *of sudden terror, nor of trouble from the wicked when it comes;*

For the Lord will be your confidence, and will keep your foot from being caught.

Do not withhold good from those to whom it is due, when it is in the power of your hand to do so.

Do not say to your neighbor, "Go, come back tomorrow and I will give it," when you have it with you.

Do not devise evil against your neighbor, for he dwells by you for safety's sake.

Do not strive with a man without cause, if he has done you no harm.

Do not envy the oppressor, and choose none of his ways.

For more Proverbs of Solomon, read one chapter per day for a month.

Trust in the Lord

BE NOT AFRAID of sudden fear, neither of the desolation of the wicked, when it cometh.
Proverbs 3:25 (KJV)

My grandmother on my father's side had a goiter (a greatly enlarged thyroid gland) just like me. Actually, hers was even bigger. When I went to see the specialist, his first words were, "How long have you had *that*?" Now we know that many diseases are genetic and can't be prevented. But in my grandmother's day, illness was equated as having sin in your life. I often wonder how she felt when people said that to her, because we all have sin in our lives.

Our Pastor says that we are an imperfect people serving a perfect God.

Many, many people have prayed for me over the years. I taught a Wednesday night Bible class to 5-year-old girls, and they prayed for me regularly. One evening during prayer time, they all voluntarily stood up and laid their hands on my throat and prayed a simple prayer of faith. I was so sure that I was healed that I immediately put my hand up to feel if it was gone. Surely their innocent and earnest prayers had done the trick. But it was still there.

One night at church, I saw my Mom's too short leg stretch out to match the length of her normal one after prayer. They prayed for me that night too, and I felt sure that my goiter would slowly shrink away. It didn't. Do I still believe in healing?

Absolutely.

Over the years I have seen and heard of many people touched by God. I don't know why it never happened to me. Sometimes only God knows and we are not to know yet. We are to trust in His understanding and not our own.

When we go through trials, we are promised that good things will come of it. Some of these good things we can see right away, some we see later and some we miss completely. Maybe it's because we don't see with the eyes of God.

Also, He sees the big picture and we only see the little world around us. He is in control of the whole universe and we are in control of nothing.

I've heard it said that we can't change our past, but we can determine our future.

Proverbs 3:25

DO NOT BE AFRAID of sudden terror, nor of trouble from the wicked when it comes. **(NKJV)**

Trust and Obey

When we walk with the Lord in the light of His Word what a glory He sheds on our way!

While we do His good will, He abides with us still, and with all who will trust and obey.

Not a shadow can rise, not a cloud in the skies, but His smile quickly drives it away;

Not a doubt or a fear, not a sigh nor a tear, can abide while we trust and obey.

Not a burden we bear, not a sorrow we share, but our toil He doth richly repay;

Not a grief nor a loss, not a frown nor a cross, but is blest if we trust and obey.

But we never can prove the delights of His love until all on the altar we lay;

For the favor He shows, and the joy He bestows, are for them who will trust and obey.

Then in fellowship sweet we will sit at His feet, or we'll walk by His side in the way;

What He says we will do, where He sends we will go—never fear, only trust and obey.

Trust and obey,

For there's no other way

To be happy in Jesus,

But to trust and obey.

John H. Sammis (1846-1919) left behind his life as a successful businessman to become a Presbyterian minister. In his later years he taught at the Bible Institute of Los Angeles. During his lifetime he wrote the lyrics (or poem) to over 100 hymns. In the case of *Trust and Obey*, the idea for the song came when a young man spoke up at a revival preached by Dwight L. Moody and said, "I don't know much about the Lord, but I do know that I need to trust Him and I need to obey Him."

FEAR NOT

#20

WAIT UPON THE LORD

"No passion so effectually robs the mind of all its powers of acting and reasoning as fear."

Edmund Burke

Ahab & Isaiah

Isaiah 7:1-17 (NIV)

When Ahaz son of Jotham, the son of Uzziah, was king of Judah, King Rezin of Aram and Pekah son of Remaliah king of Israel marched up to fight against Jerusalem, but they could not overpower it. Now the house of David was told, "Aram has allied itself with Ephraim"; so the hearts of Ahaz and his people were shaken, as the trees of the forest are shaken by the wind.

Then the Lord said to Isaiah, "Go out, you and your son Shear-Jashub, to meet Ahaz at the end of the aqueduct of the Upper Pool, on the road to the Washerman's Field. Say to him, 'Be careful and keep calm. **Do not be afraid**. *Do not lose heart because of these two smoldering stubs of firewood—because of the fierce anger of Rezin and Aram and of the son of Remaliah. They have plotted your ruin, saying, "Let us invade Judah; let us tear it apart and divide it among ourselves, and make the son of Tabeel king over it."*

Yet this is what the Sovereign Lord says:

> *"It will not take place, it will not happen, for the head of Aram is Damascus,*
>
> *and the head of Damascus is only Rezin.*
>
> *Within sixty-five years Ephraim will be too shattered to be a people.*
>
> *The head of Ephraim is Samaria, and the head of Samaria is only Remaliah's son.*
>
> *If you do not stand firm in your faith, you will not stand at all."*

Again the Lord spoke to Ahaz, "Ask the Lord your God for a sign, whether in the deepest depths or in the highest heights." But Ahaz said, "I will not ask; I will not put the Lord to the test."

Then Isaiah said, "Hear now, you house of David! Is it not enough to try the patience of men? Will you try the patience of my God also? Therefore the Lord himself will give you a sign:

"The virgin will be with child and will give birth to a son, and will call him Immanuel (God with us). He will eat curds and honey when he knows enough to reject the wrong and choose the right. But before the boy knows enough to reject the wrong and choose the right, the land of the two kings you dread will be laid waste. The Lord will bring on you and on your people and on the house of your father a time unlike any since Ephraim broke away from Judah—he will bring the king of Assyria."

For the only other mention of "Immanuel" in the Bible, please read Isaiah 8.

Wait Upon the Lord

***The Lord said, "Say unto Ahaz, 'Take heed, and be quiet: FEAR NOT, neither be fainthearted for the two tails of these smoking firebrands, for the fierce anger of Rezin with Syria.'"* Isaiah 7:4 (KJV)**

Have you ever been to an ER? If you have, you know what I mean when I mention the word, "wait."

I don't know why it takes so long. I guess there is just one doctor back there. What is he doing all of that time? It seems like they take in about one person per hour. By the time you get in there, your emergency could almost be over.

While I was waiting in the examining room this particular time, a nurse stopped by to mention that the doctor would be there in just a minute, he had to go and grab a hamburger. A hamburger? What if I'm dying here? I think the way to get their attention is to be half dead or dying. The rest can wait.

That is so typical of our society today. "Oh, I'll just do that tomorrow," or "This can wait until next week," or "I don't want to do that, let's get someone else," or "Jesus probably won't come today, so I'll think about that when I'm old." Sound familiar?

My daughter tells of a girl who came to her Driver's Ed class every day and finished-up her homework while she waited for the teacher to arrive. Every day. She knew that she had to do it, but why did she always wait until the very last minute?

One thing about surgery, it makes you face up to your mortality—right now.

Not next year, or when you're old.

When they're putting anesthetic in your IV, it's time.

How about right now? Not this afternoon or tomorrow or next week. You know He's there and you know you have to get your homework/heart work done before class starts.

How would you feel if you knocked on the pearly gates and St. Peter couldn't let you in because he went to grab a hamburger?

Isaiah 7:4

***And say to him: "Take heed, and be quiet; DO NOT FEAR or be fainthearted for these two stubs of smoking firebrands, for the fierce anger of Rezin and Aram and of the son of Remaliah.'" (NKJV)**

I Shall Not Pass This Way Again

Through this toilsome world, alas!

Once and only once I pass;

If a kindness I may show,

If a good deed I may do

To a suffering man,

Let me do it while I can.

No delay, for it is plain

I shall not pass this way again.

Author Unknown

FEAR NOT

#19

BE NOT DISMAYED

"Fear is that tax that conscience pays to guilt."

George Sewell

Israel & Jacob

Isaiah 41:1-10 (NIV)

"Be silent before me, you islands! Let the nations renew their strength!

Let them come forward and speak; let us meet together at the place of judgment.

Who has stirred up one from the east, calling him in righteousness to his service?

He hands nations over to him and subdues kings before him.

He turns them to dust with his sword, to windblown chaff with his bow.

He pursues them and moves on unscathed, by a path his feet have not traveled before.

Who has done this and carried it through, calling forth the generations from the beginning?

I, the Lord—with the first of them and with the last—I AM HE."

The islands have seen it and fear; the ends of the earth tremble.

They approach and come forward; each helps the other and says to his brother, "Be strong!"

The craftsman encourages the goldsmith,

and he who smooths with the hammer spurs on him who strikes the anvil.

He says of the welding, "It is good." He nails down the idol so it will not topple.

"But you, O Israel, my servant, Jacob, whom I have chosen, you descendants of Abraham my friend,

I took you from the ends of the earth, from its farthest corners I called you.

I said, 'You are my servant'; I have chosen you and have not rejected you.

Do not fear, *for I am with you; do not be dismayed, for I am your God.*

I will strengthen you and help you; I will uphold you with my righteous right hand."

"I Am He" is mentioned 16 times in the Bible. Jesus said it in John 18:8

Be Not Dismayed

The Lord said, "FEAR THOU NOT; for I am with thee: be not dismayed; for I am thy God; I will strengthen thee; yea, I will help thee; yea, I will uphold thee with the right hand of my righteousness."
Isaiah 41:10 (KJV)

I know that I know that I know that God is God.

In fact, my life verse is from 2 Timothy 1:12: *"Yet I am not ashamed, because I know whom I have believed, and am convinced that He is able to guard what I have entrusted to Him for that day."* (NIV)

I cannot prove this, I only know it by faith. We have the Bible, we have archeological finds, and we have miracles. But how can you prove faith?

You live it.

You struggle, you triumph and God gives you peace and joy. You sleep at night without guilt. You feel sorry for those who suffer. You feel sorry for those who don't trust in Him. We love our enemies and those who despitefully use us. We learn to turn the other cheek.

Whoa, wait a minute! How can you like someone who is mean to you?

I didn't say "like," I said "love."

In every hospital I visited over these twelve months, almost all of my nurses were compassionate, caring, thoughtful and polite. All but one--she was a bear. Grouchy, thoughtless, rough and rude.

I always made it a point to learn the name of each of my nurses and I tried to thank them often. I did the same with the mean one, but she was still mean.

Later I found out from a friend who knew her that she was going through a very bad situation in her marriage. Did her attitude change? Not while I was there.

I was commanded to lover her without the consequence of her changing.

I wasn't to love her to make her change—I was just to love her.

Isaiah 41:10

So DO NOT FEAR for I am with you; do not be dismayed, for I am your God. I will strengthen you and help you; I will uphold you with my righteous right hand." (NIV)

I Know Whom I Have Believed

I know not why God's wondrous grace to me He has made known,

Nor why—unworthy as I am—He claimed me for His own.

I know not how this saving faith to me He did impart.

Nor how believing in His Word wrought peace within my heart.

I know not how the Spirit moves, convincing men of sin,

Revealing Jesus through the Word, creating faith in Him.

I know not what of good or ill may be reserved for me,

Of weary ways of golden days, before His face I see.

I know not when my Lord may come, at night or noonday fair,

Nor if I'll walk the vale with Him, or "meet Him in the air."

But I know Whom I have believed,

And am persuaded that He is able

To keep that which I've committed

Unto Him against that day.

Daniel Webster Whittle (1840-1901) was a major in the American Civil War as well as a poet, hymn writer and Bible teacher. He later became an evangelist associated with Dwight L. Moody and the Great Evangelistic Movement in the late 1800's. Mr. Whittle wrote over 200 hymns. This one is based on my favorite Bible verse—2 Timothy 1:12.

The Love Chapter

If I speak in the tongues of men and of angels,

But have not LOVE,

I am only a resounding gong or a clanging cymbal.

If I have the gift of prophecy

And can fathom all mysteries and all knowledge,

And if I have a faith that can move mountains,

But have not LOVE,

I am nothing.

If I give all I possess to the poor

And surrender my body to the flames,

But have not LOVE,

I gain nothing.

LOVE is patient,

LOVE is kind.

It does not envy,

It does not boast,

It is not proud.

It is not rude,

It is not self-seeking,

It is not easily angered,

It keeps no record of wrongs.

LOVE does not delight in evil,

But rejoices with the truth.

It always protects,

Always trusts,

Always hopes,

Always perseveres.

LOVE never fails.

But where there are prophecies,

They will cease;

Where there are tongues,

They will be stilled;

Where there is knowledge,

It will pass away.

For we know in part

And we prophesy in part,

But when perfection comes,

The imperfect disappears.

When I was a child,

I talked like a child.

I thought like a child,

I reasoned like a child.

When I became a man,

I put childish ways behind me.

Now we see but a poor reflection

As in a mirror;

Then we shall see face to face.

Now I know in part;

Then I shall know fully.

Even as I am fully known.

And now these three things remain:

Faith, Hope and LOVE.

But the greatest of these is LOVE.

1 Corinthians 13 (NIV)

Apostle Paul (AD 5--AD 67) wrote this epistle to the church at Corinth in the country of Greece. He also wrote Romans, Second Corinthians, Galatians, Ephesians, Philippians, Colossians, First & Second Thessalonians, Hebrews, First & Second Timothy, Titus and Philemon—most of the New Testament, in fact. In his early years, Saul of Tarsus actually persecuted and killed many Christians until God miraculously saved him on the Road to Damascus.

FEAR NOT

#18

HE WILL HELP

"Look not mournfully into the past. It comes not back again. Wisely improve the present.

It is thine. Go forth to meet the shadowy future without fear."

Henry Wadsworth Longfellow

Poor & Needy

Isaiah 41:11-20 (NIV)

"All who rage against you will surely be ashamed and disgraced;

Those who oppose you will be as nothing and perish.

Though you search for your enemies, you will not find them.

Those who wage war against you will be as nothing at all.

For I am the Lord, your God, who takes hold of your right hand and says to you,

Do not fear.

Do not be afraid, *O worm Jacob, O little Israel, for I myself will help you,"*

Declares the Lord, your Redeemer, the Holy One of Israel.

See, I will make you into a threshing sledge, new and sharp, with many teeth.

You will thresh the mountains and crush them, and reduce the hills to chaff.

You will winnow them, the wind will pick them up, and a gale will blow them away.

But you will rejoice in the Lord and glory in the Holy One of Israel.

The poor and needy search for water, but there is none; their tongues are parched with thirst.

But I the Lord will answer them; I, the God of Israel, will not forsake them.

I will make rivers flow on barren heights, and springs within the valleys.

I will turn the desert into pools of water and the parched ground into springs.

I will put in the desert the cedar and the acacia, the myrtle and the olive.

I will set pines in the wasteland, the fir and the cypress together.

So that people may see and know, may consider and understand,

That the hand of the Lord has done this, that the Holy One of Israel has created it."

For David's praise of the Holy One, please read Psalm 71.

He Will Help

The Lord said: "FEAR NOT, thou worm Jacob, and ye men of Israel; I will help thee, saith the Lord, and they Redeemer, the Holy One of Israel." Isaiah 41:14 (NIV)

This verse reminds me of the children's song: "Jesus loves me, this I know, for the Bible tells me so. Little ones to Him belong, we are weak, but He is strong."

Without Him, we are nothing. We have no strength to fight any battles. Oh, yes, we can muddle through a little while in our own weak way, but we are more that conquerors through Christ Jesus.

It's not enough just to win the battle—we must win the battle for the right reason. Obviously I'm talking about spiritual battles here. Every day, no matter what happens, or how unkind someone is to us, we can have the victory. Not on our own, of course, but only with His strength.

If we do not put our hurts behind us, bitterness will grow.

Baggage will pile up.

Lives will be destroyed.

Generations will be affected.

I've always wondered what that verse meant that says: *"And the sin of the fathers will be visited on their sons and their son's sons, even unto the fifth generation."* Numbers 14:18 (NIV)

I think that this refers to unresolved hurts and the resulting bitterness. You treat others differently when you carry baggage. Then your child has baggage from you and treats his/her spouse and children differently because of it.

We all sin and get hurt.

The secret is to give it to Jesus—forgive your offender and forget it—even if they don't ask for your forgiveness. A friend I know calls it "catch and release." If you hear it and it hurts or offends you, let it go immediately, don't even think about it again.

Holding grudges will eat you alive from the inside out, just like a worm.

Isaiah 41:14

"DO NOT BE AFRAID, O worm, Jacob, O little Israel, for I myself will help you," declares the Lord, your Redeemer, the Holy One of Israel." **(NIV)**

Jesus Loves Me!

Jesus loves me! This I know, for the Bible tells me so.

Little ones to Him belong; they are weak, but He is strong.

Jesus loves me! He will stay close beside me all the way:

Thou hast died and bled for me, I will henceforth live for Thee.

Jesus loves me! Loves me still, though I'm very weak and ill;

That I might from sin be free; bled and died upon the tree.

Jesus loves me! He who died, Heaven's gate to open wide;

He will wash away my sin; let His little child come in.

Yes, Jesus loves me!

Yes, Jesus loves me!

Yes, Jesus loves me!

The Bible tells me so.

Anna and Susan Warner began a writing career after the death of their father in 1857. Left alone, they turned to fiction-writing to support themselves. Their first book, *The Wide, Wide World*, was almost as popular as *Uncle Tom's Cabin*. But it was the little-known book, *Say and Seal*, that sealed their fate. In the story, a man visits the bedside of a dying child. The little one is very fearful and the man quotes a simple poem to comfort him. The poem was *Jesus Loves Me!* and it did comfort the child as he died. When William B. Bradbury, a great hymn writer, read the book, he saw potential in the simple verse and composed a melody to go with the words. The song spread from the battlefields of the Civil War to churches all across America. Then missionaries took the song around the world.

FEAR NOT

#17

I AM WITH YOU

"Never let the fear of striking out get in your way."

Babe Ruth

You Are Mine

Isaiah 43:1-12 (NIV)

But now, this is what the Lord says—he who created you, O Jacob, he who formed you, O Israel:

*"**Fear not**, for I have redeemed you; I have summoned you by name; you are mine.*

When you pass through the waters, I will be with you;

And when you pass through the rivers, they will not sweep over you.

When you walk through the fire, you will not be burned; the flames will not set you ablaze.

For I am the Lord, your God, the Holy One of Israel, your Savior;

I give Egypt for your ransom, Cush and Seba in your stead.

Since you are precious and honored in my sight, and because I love you.

I will give men in exchange for you, and people in exchange for your life.

***Do not be afraid**, for I am with you; I will bring your children from the east and you from the west.*

I will say to the north, 'Give them up!' and to the south, 'Do not hold them back.'

Bring my sons from afar and my daughters from the ends of the earth—

Everyone who is called by my name, whom I created for my glory, whom I formed and made."

Lead out those who have eyes but are blind, who have ears but are deaf.

Let them bring in their witnesses to prove they were right, so that others may hear and say, "It is true."

"You are my witnesses," declares the Lord, "and my servant whom I have chosen,

so that you may know and believe me and understand that I am He.

Before me no god was formed, nor will there be one after me.

I, even I, am the Lord, and apart from me there is no savior."

To see how we are "fearfully and wonderfully" made, please read Psalm 139.

I Am With You

The Lord said, "FEAR NOT: for I am with thee: I will bring thy seed from the east, and gather thee from the west, I will say to the north, 'Give up,' and to the south, 'Keep not back: bring my sons from afar, and my daughters from the ends of the earth.'" Isaiah 43:5 (KJV)

We are His witnesses; which means we are to witness to others about His great love.

He loved us so much that He sent His only Son.

His only Son loved us so much that He gave His life for us.

Would I be willing to actually die for someone else?

I heard a story about a missionary who was commanded to deny Christ or they would kill his family and then him.

He looked at his wife and ten children and said, "I will see you soon in Heaven."

John Rogers, the first Christian martyr to be burned at the stake by Queen Mary, left a long, final letter to his children in 1555. One of the things he stated in that letter was:

> ***"Be never proud by any means, build not your house too high,***
> ***But always have before your eyes, that you are born to die."***

Why do we cling so fiercely to the things of this earth?

Our time here on this spinning globe is but a breath compared to an eternity with God in Heaven. Other things won't matter there, only Jesus. The only thing we should be concerned about is collecting and keeping souls.

Isaiah 43:5

DO NOT BE AFRAID, for I am with you: I will bring your children from the east and gather you from the west. I will say to the north, "Give them up!" and to the south, "Do not hold them back!" Bring my sons from afar and my daughters from the ends of the earth. (NIV)

From John Rogers to His Children

Give ear my children to my words whom God hath dearly bought,
Lay up His laws within your heart, and print them in your thoughts.
I leave you here a little book for you to look upon,
That you may see your father's face when he is dead and gone:
Who for the hope of heavenly things, while he did here remain,
Gave over all his golden years to prison and to pain.
Where I, among my iron bands, enclosed in the dark
Not many days before my death, I did compose this work;
And for example to your youth, to whom I wish all good,
I send you here God's perfect truth, and seal it with my blood.
To you my heirs of earthly things: which I do leave behind,
That you may read and understand and keep it in your minds.
That as you have been heirs of that that once shall wear away,
You also may possess that part, which never shall decay.
Keep always God before your eyes, with all your whole intent,
Commit no sin in any wise, keep His commandment
Abhor that arrant whore of Rome, and her blasphemies,
And drink not of her cursed cup, obey not her decrees.

Give honor to your mother dear, remember well her pain,
And recompense her in her age, with the like love again.
Be always ready for her help, and let her not decay,
Remember well your father all, who would have been your stay.
Give of your portion to the poor, as riches do arise,
And from the needy naked soul, turn not away your eyes:
For he that doth not hear the cry of those that stand in need,
Shall cry himself and not be heard, when he does hope to speed.
If God hath given you increase, and blessed well your store,
Remember you are put in trust, and should relieve the poor.
Beware of foul and filthy lust, let such things have no place,
Keep clean your vessels in the Lord, that He may you embrace.
Ye are the temples of the Lord, for you are dearly bought,
And they that do defile the same, shall surely come to naught.
Be never proud by any means, build not your house too high.
But always have before your eyes, that you are born to die.

Defraud not him that hired is, your labor to sustain,
But pay him still without delay, his wages for his pain.
And as you would that other men against you should proceed,
Do you the same to them again, when they do stand in need.
Impart your portion to the poor, in money and in meat
And send the feeble fainting soul, of that which you do eat.
Ask counsel always of the wise, give ear unto the end,
And ne'er refuse the sweet rebuke of him that is thy friend.
Be always thankful to the Lord, with prayer and with praise,
Begging of Him to bless your work, and to direct your ways.

Seek first, I say, the living God, and always Him adore,
And then be sure that He will bless, your basket and your store.
And I beseech Almighty God, replenish you with grace,
That I may meet you in the heavens, and see you face to face.
And though the fire my body burns, contrary to my kind,
That I cannot enjoy your love according to my mind:
Yet I do hope that when the heavens shall vanish like a scroll,
I shall see you in perfect shape, in body and soul.
And that I may enjoy your love, and you enjoy the land,
I do beseech the living Lord, to hold you in His hand.
Though here my body be adjudged in flaming fire to fry,

My soul I trust, will straight ascend to live with God on High.
What though this carcass smart awhile what though this life decay,
My soul I hope will be with God, and live with Him for aye.
I know I am a sinner born, from the original,
And that I do deserve to die by my forefather's fall:
But by our Savior's precious blood, which on the cross was spilt,
Who freely offered up his life, to save our souls from guilt:
I hope redemption I shall have, and all who in Him trust,
When I shall see him face to face, and live among the just.
Why then should I fear death's grim look since Christ for me did die,
For King and Caesar; rich and poor, the force of death must try.

When I am chained to the stake, and faggots girt me round,
Then pray the Lord my soul in heaven may be with glory crowned.
Come welcome death the end of fears, I am prepared to die:
Those earthly flames will send my soul up to the Lord on high.
Farewell my children to the world, where you must yet remain;
The Lord of hosts be your defense, 'till we do meet again.
Farewell my true and loving wife, my children and my friends,
I hope in heaven to see you all, when all things have their end.
If you go on to serve the Lord, as you have now begun,
You shall walk safely all your days, until your life be done.
God grant you so to end your days, as He shall think is best,
That I may meet you in the heavens, where I do hope to rest.

John Rogers, a minister in London, was the first martyr in the reign of Queen Mary, being burned at the stake in 1554. He wrote this letter/poem to his wife and ten children just a few days before his death. What he didn't know was that they all followed him to the stake and soon joined him in heaven.

FEAR NOT

#16

CHOSEN ONE

"Expose yourself to your deepest fear; after that, fear has no power,

And the fear of freedom shrinks and vanishes. You are free.

Jim Morrison

Alpha & Omega

Isaiah 44:1-8 (NIV)

"But now listen, O Jacob, my servant, Israel, whom I have chosen.

This is what the Lord says—He who made you, who formed you in the womb, and who will help you:

***Do not be afraid**, O Jacob, my servant, Jeshurun whom I have chosen.*

For I will pour water on the thirsty land, and streams on the dry ground;

I will pour out my Spirit on your offspring, and my blessing on your descendants.

They will spring up like grass in a meadow, like poplar trees by flowing streams.

One will say, 'I belong to the Lord'; another will call himself by the name of Jacob;

Still another will write on his hand, 'The Lord's,' and will not take the name Israel.

This is what the Lord says—Israel's King and Redeemer, the Lord Almighty:

I am the first and I am the last (Alpha & Omega); apart from me there is no God.

Who then is like me? Let him proclaim it. Let him declare and lay out before me

What has happened since I established my ancient people,

And what is yet to come—yes, let him foretell what will come.

*Do not tremble. **Do not be afraid.** Did I not proclaim this and foretell it long ago?*

You are my witnesses. Is there any God besides me?

No, there is no other Rock; I know not one."

For more on Alpha & Omega, please read Revelation 1:21 & 22.

*(**"Alpha"** is the first letter of the Greek alphabet and **"Omega"** is the last)*

The Chosen One

Thus saith the Lord that made thee, and formed thee from the womb, which will help thee: "FEAR NOT, O Jacob, my servant; and thou, (Israel), whom I have chosen." Isaiah 44:2 (KJV)

I walked into Pre-Op at a major university hospital with my husband, my children, my mother, my Pastor and his dear wife. It was early in the morning and the first thing we saw was a giant white board on the wall before us. On the left hand side were about thirty patient names and the time of their morning surgeries.

My surgery was scheduled for the afternoon. On the right hand side of the giant white board was only one name.

My name.

The entire afternoon was reserved for me only.

I knew that my surgery was rather risky—I had to bring a living will with me or they wouldn't undertake it. But this really gave me pause.

I cried out to the Rock of my Salvation.

He who formed me in the womb. He who formed my children in the womb and will form my children's children.

He chose me to be in this place for a reason. He knows all of my yesterdays and He will be with me in all of my tomorrows, if this surgery proves a success.

All of my family and church and town were praying for me and I didn't want to give in to fear. And so I decided that I was special; I was chosen.

Today is the day and I am ready.

Isaiah 44:2

This is what the Lord says—He Who made you, who formed you in the womb, and who will help you: "DO NOT BE AFRAID, O Jacob, my servant, whom I have chosen." (NIV)

Red Geraniums

Life did not bring me silken gowns,

Nor jewels for my hair,

Nor signs of gabled foreign towns

In distant countries fair,

But I can glimpse beyond my pane, a green and friendly hill,

And red geraniums aflame upon my windowsill.

The brambled cares of everyday,

The tiny humdrum things,

May bind my feet when they would stray,

But still my heart has wings.

While red geraniums are bloomed against my window glass,

And low above my green-sweet hill the gypsy wind clouds pass.

And if my dreamings ne'er come true,

The brightest and the best,

But leave me lone my journey through,

I'll set my heart at rest,

And thank God for home-sweet things, a green and friendly hill,

And red geraniums aflame upon my window will.

Martha Haskell Clark

FEAR NOT

#15

NO OTHER GODS

"The only thing we have to fear is fear itself."

Franklin Delano Roosevelt

King & Redeemer

Isaiah 44:8-17 (NIV)

*"Do not tremble. **Do not be afraid.** Did I not proclaim this and foretell it long ago?*

You are my witnesses. Is there no other God besides me?

No, there is no other Rock; I know not one."

All who make idols are nothing, and the things they treasure are worthless.

Who shapes a god and casts an idol, which can profit him nothing?

Let them all come together and take their stand; they will be brought down to terror and infamy.

The blacksmith takes a tool and works with it in the coals;

He shapes an idol with hammers, he forges it with the might of his arm.

The carpenter measures with a line and makes an outline with a marker;

He roughs it out with chisels and marks it with compasses;

He shapes it in the form of man, of man in all his glory, that it may dwell in a shrine.

He cut down cedars, or perhaps took a cypress or oak.

He let it grow among the trees of the forest, or planted a pine, and the rain made it grow.

It is man's fuel for burning; some of it he takes and warms himself, he kindles a fire and bakes bread.

But he also fashions a god and worships it; he makes an idol and bows down to it.

Half of the wood he burns in the fire; over it he prepares his meal, he roasts his meat and eats his fill.

He also warms himself and says, "Ah! I am warm; I see the fire."

From the rest he makes a god, his idol; he bows down to it and worships.

He prays to it and says, "Save me; you are my god!"

For more on the Rock, read David's last words in 2 Samuel 23:1-7.

No Other Gods

***FEAR YE NOT, NEITHER BE AFRAID:** have not I told thee from that time, and have declared it? Ye are even my witnesses. Is there a God beside me? Yea, there is no God; I know not any.* Isaiah 44:8 (KJV)

The days were counting down to my first surgery. Two days before I was to go in, the doctor's office called me at home in a panic. "Your insurance company just contacted us and said that they're not going to cover this! Do you still want to go ahead with it?"

I turned to my husband and he said, "Yes, you have to have this done. We'll worry about paying for it later."

After I hung up, I called my insurance company. Between the two phone calls, an unheard of earthquake struck Seattle and I was unable to reach them.

This meant that I would have to file an appeal within six weeks after my surgery--while I was supposed to be recuperating and may not feel well enough to do it.

After twenty years of waiting to be eligible for this coverage, it all fell apart in a matter of moments. So now, we could trust in man's ways no longer—we had to rely totally on Him.

When you think about it, man's work is puny work indeed. Really pathetic compared to a God who fashioned the entire universe.

Just look at how amazingly complex a single cell is (and we have 50 TRILLION of them!).

I've read that if a scientist studies evolution long enough, he will reach the conclusion that a Higher Power had a hand in the miraculous creation of this world.

They call it "Intelligent Design." I call Him **"Elohim"** (God of Creation).

Why do we rely on man when God is right there the whole time?

How did the appeal work out? Oh, they had made a clerical error and the surgery was covered after all.

Isaiah 44:8

*Do not tremble, **DO NOT BE AFRAID**. Did I not proclaim this and foretell it long ago? You are my witnesses. Is there any God besides me? No, there is no other Rock; I know not one.* **(NIV)**

Rock of Ages

Rock of Ages, cleft for me, let me hid myself in Thee;

Let the water and the blood, from Thy wounded side which flowed,

Be of sin the double cure, save from wrath and make me pure.

Not the labor of my hands can fulfill Thy law's demands;

Could my zeal no respite know, could my tears forever flow,

All for sin could not atone; Thou must save and Thou alone.

Nothing in my hand I bring, simply to Thy cross I cling;

Naked, come to Thee for dress; helpless, look to Thee for grace;

Foul, I to the fountain fly; wash me, Savior, or I die.

While I draw this fleeting breath, when my eyes shall close in death,

When I rise to worlds unknown, and behold Thee on Thy throne,

Rock of Ages, cleft for me, let me hide myself in Thee.

Augustus Montague Toplady (1740-1778) was a preacher born in Surrey, England. Traveling home one night, he was caught in a vicious thunderstorm and took shelter beneath a gigantic rock in the gorge of Burrington Combe. It is now officially called the "Rock of Ages" on local maps and a nearby tea shop is named after it. Someday I would like to go and see that rock.

FEAR NOT

#14

EVERLASTING SALVATION

"Never fear spoiling children by making them too happy.

Happiness is the atmosphere in which all good affections grow."

Ann E. Bray

Zion & Eden

Isaiah 51:1-8 (NIV)

"Listen to me, you who pursue righteousness and who seek the Lord:

Look to the Rock from which you were cut and to the quarry from which you were hewn;

Look to Abraham, your father, and to Sarah, who gave you birth.

When I called him he was but one, and I blessed him and made him many.

The Lord will surely comfort Zion and will look with compassion on all her ruins;

He will make her deserts like Eden, her wastelands like the garden of the Lord.

Joy and gladness will be found in her, thanksgiving and the sound of singing.

Listen to me, my people; hear me, my nation:

The law will go out from me; my justice will become a light to the nations.

My righteousness draws near speedily, my salvation is on the way, and my arm will bring justice.

The islands will look to me and wait in hope for my arm.

Lift up your eyes to the heavens, look at the earth beneath;

The heavens will vanish like smoke, the earth will wear out like a garment; its inhabitants die like flies.

But my salvation will last forever, my righteousness will never fail.

Hear me, you who know what is right, you people who have my law in your hearts:

Do not fear *the reproach of men or be terrified by their insults.*

For the moth will eat them up like a garment; the worm will devour them like wool.

But my righteousness will last forever, my salvation through all generations."

For the story of Abram and Sarai, please read Genesis 11 & 12.

Everlasting Salvation

Harken unto me, ye that know righteousness, the people in whose heart is my law; FEAR YE NOT the reproach of men, neither be ye afraid of their reviling. Isaiah 51:7 (KJV)

I recently read a novel about a young girl who was kidnapped and murdered. Her father's faith was challenged by this. He was angry and doubted God. But God spoke to his heart and shared with him that He had been with his daughter during her time of great need, and had comforted her as she died.

The father knew that he would see her again in Heaven someday, but he wanted to know why his innocent child had to suffer so.

They say that children who die young are like visiting angels.

But why do they have to suffer, God?

I never did understand why children get cancer. My cousin, Valerie, who was the same age as me, died when she was only four years old from a type of leukemia that is curable today. My aunt and uncle donated her body to science, so maybe she had a hand in curing what took her life.

No one deserves to suffer.

We suffer because of sin.

Not our own sin, but because sin is in the world. My granddaughter was so disappointed that Adam and Eve sinned in the Garden and ruined a perfect world. I told her that someone else would have done it anyway—we all sin every day, don't we?

Just as suffering isn't dependent on our goodness, neither is salvation dependent on our goodness.

It's a free gift from Him to us.

And if you're suffering, He has another free gift.

Comfort.

He will be there with you as you go through it.

Isaiah 51:7

Hear me, you who know what is right, you people who have my laws in your hearts; DO NOT FEAR the reproach of men or be terrified by their insults." (NIV)

Get a Transfer

If you are on the Gloomy Line,

Get a transfer.

If you're inclined to fret and pine,

Get a transfer.

Get off the track of doubt and gloom,

Get on the Sunshine Track—there's room—

Get a transfer.

If you're on the Worry Train,

Get a transfer.

You must not stay there and complain,

Get a transfer.

The Cheerful Cars are passing through,

And there's lots of room for you—

Get a transfer.

If you're on the Grouchy Track,

Get a transfer.

Just take a Happy Special back,

Get a transfer.

Jump on the train and pull the rope,

That lands you at the station Hope—

Get a transfer.

Author Unknown

FEAR NOT

#13

FUTURE GLORY

"Present fears are less than horrible imaginings."

William Shakespeare

Days of Noah

Isaiah 54:1-13 (NIV)

"Sing, O barren woman, you who never bore a child;

Burst into song, shout for joy, you who were never in labor;

Because more are the children of a desolate woman than of her who has a husband.

Enlarge the place of your tent, stretch your tent curtains wide, do not hold back.

Lengthen your cords, strengthen your stakes, for you will spread out to the right and to the left.

Your descendants will dispossess nations and settle in their desolate cities.

Do not be afraid*; you will not suffer shame.*

Do not fear *disgrace; you will not be humiliated.*

You will forget the shame of your youth and remember no more the reproach of your widowhood.

For your Maker is your husband—the Lord Almighty is His name.

The Holy One of Israel is your Redeemer; He is called the God of all the earth.

The Lord will call you back as if you were a wife deserted and distressed in spirit.

A wife who married young, only to be rejected.

For a brief moment I abandoned you, but with deep compassion I will bring you back.

In a surge of anger I hid my face from you for a moment, but with everlasting kindness

I will have compassion on you," says the Lord your Redeemer.

"To me this is like the days of Noah, when I swore that the waters would never again cover the earth.

So now I have sworn not to be angry with you, never to rebuke you again.

Though the mountains be shaken and the hills removed."

For the story of Noah and the flood, please read Genesis 5-9.

Future Glory

FEAR NOT; for thou shalt not be ashamed: neither be thou confounded; for thou shalt not be put to shame: for thou shalt forget the shame of thy youth, and shalt not remember the reproach of thy widowhood any more. Isaiah 54:4 (KJV)

"What is Heaven like?" the grandkids asked, so I read to them from Revelation 21. Streets of gold, gates of pearl, mansions and angels—but most of all, my Best Friend, Jesus.

***"The city does not need the sun or the moon to shine on it,
for the glory of God gives it light."*** Revelation 21:23 (NIV)

Every Christian should be looking forward to Heaven, but not to the point of rejecting this life here below. We are to occupy until He comes.

Think of it as longing for a vacation or a special occasion to come to pass. We still live out every day to the best of our ability, but, oh, we look forward to that glorious time ahead!

The best thing about Heaven compared to a vacation, is that our time in Heaven never comes to an end. I still have trouble picturing eternity in this finite world, don't you?

The first time I went under anesthetic, it reminded me of how quickly we will be translated into His presence. When they began administering it to me, I was wide awake.

The very next instant to me, it was over and I was waking up—like the twinkling of an eye.

That feeling of full consciousness followed immediately by complete oblivion was weird.

When I began to wake up, I heard the recovery room nurse humming and it reminded me of my daughter. But I knew I wasn't in Heaven because I didn't see the *Light of the World*.

Isaiah 54:4

DO NOT BE AFRAID; you will not suffer shame. DO NOT FEAR disgrace; you will not be humiliated. You will forget the shame of your youth and remember no more the reproach of your widowhood. **(NIV)**

Changed in the Twinkling of an Eye

When the trump of the great archangel its mighty tone shall sound,
And the end of the age proclaiming, shall pierce the depths profound;
When the Son of Man shall come in His glory to take the saints on high,
What a shouting in the skies from the multitudes that rise,
Changed in the twinkling of an eye.

When He comes in the clouds descending, and they who loved Him here,
From their graves shall awake and praise Him with joy and not with fear;
When the body and the soul are united, and clothed no more to die,
What a shouting there will be when each other's face we see.
Changed in the twinkling of an eye.

O the seed that was sown in weakness shall then be raised in power
And the songs of the blood bought millions shall hail that blissful hour;
When we gather safely home in the morning, and night's dark shadows fly,
What a shouting on the shore when we meet to part no more,
Changed in the twinkling of an eye.

Changed in the twinkling of any eye,
Changed in the twinkling of an eye,
The trumpet shall sound,
The dead shall be raised,
Changed in the twinkling of an eye.

Frances Jane (Fanny) Crosby (1820-1915) was one of the most prolific hymn writers in the world. After a simple cold and inflammation of the eyes left her blind, she went on to write over 8,000 songs and hymns in her lifetime. This hymn is based on the verse in *1 Corinthians 15:51*. At the age of 38 she married Alexander Van Alstyne, Jr. and a year later they had a daughter, Frances. Sadly, she died shortly after from Sudden Infant Death Syndrome.

FEAR NOT

#12

RIGHTEOUSNESS

"We promise according to our hopes and perform according to our fears."

Author Unknown

New Jerusalem

Isaiah 54:11-17 (NIV)

Isaiah 55:8-11 (NIV)

"O afflicted city, lashed by storms and not comforted,

I will build you with stones of turquoise, your foundations with sapphires.

I will make your battlements of rubies, your gates of sparkling jewels, and your walls of precious stones.

All your sons will be taught by the Lord, and great will be your children's peace.

In righteousness you will be established: tyranny will be far from you;

You will have nothing to fear.

Terror will be far removed, it will not come near you. If anyone does attack you,

It will not be my doing; whoever attacks you will surrender to you.

See, it is I who created the blacksmith who fans the coals into flame and forges a weapon.

And it is I who has created the destroyer to work havoc.

No weapon forged against you will prevail, and you will refute every tongue that accuses you.

This is the heritage of the servants of the Lord, and this is their vindication from me," declares the Lord.

"As the heavens are higher than the earth, so are my ways higher than your ways,

And my thoughts than your thoughts.

As the rain and the snow come down from heaven,

And do not return to it without watering the earth and making it bud and flourish,

So that it yields seed for the sower and bread for the eater,

So is my word that goes out from my mouth: It will not return to me empty,

But will accomplish what I desire and achieve the purpose for which I sent it."

For more splendors of Heaven, please read Revelation 21.

Righteousness

In righteousness shalt thou be established: thou shalt be far from oppression; FOR THOU SHALT NOT FEAR: and from terror; for it shall not come near thee. Isaiah 54:14 (KJV)

I just want to take a moment to thank God for all of the doctors and nurses and hospitals that our country is so richly blessed with. I see magazine advertisements all the time that show children in third world countries who desperately need surgery, but there is no medical help available.

Lord, bless those doctors, nurses and optometrists who go on medical missions trips to help them!

My brother worked at a missionary hospital in a remote mountainous area of Papua New Guinea for six years and he said that you could not believe the long lines of people who would come to that hospital every single day.

Unfortunately, they had to travel long distances on foot to get there and either they started out too late or it took too long, because many of the cases were beyond help.

While people waited to see the doctors, they showed them the *"Jesus"* film and many were brought to the saving grace of the Lord before they met the saving grace of the doctors.

It was hard on my family when my brother, his wife, and two young children sacrificed hearth and home to minister on the other side of the world. But every missionary leaves behind family and friends.

If they didn't go, how would the world come to know about Jesus?

If doctors didn't spend years training for their profession and give up many sleepless nights to minister to us who need them, how would we live?

My niece is now preparing to go to Papua New Guinea herself as a doctor.

What comfort am I willing to give up for righteousness?

Isaiah 54:14

In righteousness you will be established; tyranny will be far from you; you will have NOTHING TO FEAR. Terror will be far removed; it will not come near you. **(NIV)**

Papua New Guinea Bible Verses

Krais,

I bin givim bel belong em long yumi,

Na oltaim em I mekim yumi win tru.

Romans 8:37 (Pidgin English)

Yet in all these things we are more than conquerors through Him who loved us.
Romans 8:37 (NKJV)

Yurela I mas sanar strong long Bikpela.

Olsem diwai I sanar strong long graun.

Kolosi 2:7 (Pidgin English)

Rooted and built up in him and established in the faith, as you have been taught.
Colossians 2:7 (NKJV)

Papua New Guinea is just north of Australia and was first settled around the shore. It wasn't until the 1960's that gold prospectors found another civilization living on the mountaintops. It is estimated that only 18% of the population lives in cities, the rest are very primitive, with grass huts and dirt floors. New Guineans in the Western Highland Province who have been saved, reproduce their Bible on bark that they chew to soften. They letter it and sell it to tourists. There are over 841 different language groups and many of the indigenous plants and animals have never even been classified.

FEAR NOT

#11

FREEDOM

"Fear not that life shall come to an end, but rather fear that it shall never have a beginning."

John Henry Cardinal Newman

Jeremiah & Gedaliah

Jeremiah 40:1-10 (NKJV)

The word that came to Jeremiah from the Lord after Nebuzaradan the captain of the guard had let him go from Ramah, when he had taken him bound in chains among all who were carried away captive from Jerusalem and Judah, who were carried away captive to Babylon.

And the captain of the guard took Jeremiah and said to him:

"The Lord your God has pronounced this doom on this place. Now the Lord has brought it, and has done just as he said. Because you people have sinned against the Lord, and not obeyed his voice, therefore this thing has come upon you.

"And now look, I free you this day from the chains that were on your hand. If it seems good to you to come with me to Babylon, come, and I will look after you. But if it seems wrong for you to come with me to Babylon, remain here. See, all the land is before you; wherever it seems good and convenient for you to go, go there."

Now while Jeremiah had not yet gone back, Nebuzaradan said,

"Go back to Gedaliah the son of Ahikam, the son of Shaphan, whom the king of Babylon has made governor over the cities of Judah, and dwell with him among the people. Or go wherever it seems convenient for you to go."

So the captain of the guard gave him rations and a gift and let him go. Then Jeremiah went to Gedaliah the son of Ahikam, to Mizpah, and dwelt with him among the people who were left in the land.

And when all the captains of the armies who were in the fields, they and their men, heard that the king of Babylon had made Gedaliah the son of Ahikam governor in the land, and had committed to him men, women, children, and the poorest of the land who had not been carried away captive to Babylon, then they came to Gedaliah at Mizpah.

And Gedaliah the son of Ahikam, took an oath before them and their men, saying, **"Do not be afraid** *to serve the Chaldeans. Dwell in the land and serve the king of Babylon, and it shall be well with you.*

As for me, I will indeed dwell at Mizpah and serve the Chaldeans who come to us. But you, gather wine and summer fruit and oil, put them in your vessels, and dwell in your cities that you have taken."

For more of the story about Jeremiah, please read Jeremiah 26.

Freedom

And Gedaliah the son of Ahikam, swore unto them and to their men, saying, "FEAR NOT to serve the Chaldeans: dwell in the land, and serve the king of Babylon, and it shall be well with thee."
Jeremiah 40:9 (KJV)

I once heard someone say that all fear is tied to our fear of death. Think about it: loss of job, no money, starvation; illness, sickness, death; fear of flying; fear of falling; fear of choking; fear of snakes; fear of water; fear of divorce; fear of birth; fear of death.

It's all the same thing, or leads to the same thing anyway.

When you're really ready for surgery, or any other very scary thing, you will be able to say this and really believe it: "If I wake up, that's okay. If I don't wake up, that's okay too."

When you reach this point, you are ready for life as well as death.

That's what we are all about, isn't it? This short time on earth is nothing compared to an eternity in Heaven or hell. I'm not saying that you're going to die because of this surgery, or whatever it is that you are facing, but you could, and I hope that you are ready to face death.

Believing that dying is okay and having no fear is because you know where you're going.

Not knowing causes the fear.

Do you know where you are going when this life is through? You *can* know and you *can* overcome the fear. I did.

"For the wages of sin is death, but the gift of God is eternal life through Jesus Christ our Lord."
Romans 6:23 (NIV)

This is my son's favorite Bible verse and you can use it to ask Him to take away your fear.

Jeremiah 40:9

Gedaliah son of Ahikam, took an oath to reassure them and their men. "DO NOT BE AFRAID to serve the Babylonians," he said. "Settle down in the land and serve the king of Babylon, and it will go well with you." **(NIV)**

Worthwhile

It is easy enough to be pleasant, when life flows by like a song,

But the man worthwhile is one who will smile, when everything goes dead wrong.

For the test of the heart is trouble, and it always comes with the years,

And the smile that is worth the praises of earth

Is the smile that shines through tears.

It is easy enough to be prudent, when nothing tempts you to stray,

When without or within no voices of sin is luring your soul away;

But it's only a negative virtue until it is tried by fire,

And the life that is worth the honor on earth

Is the one that resists desire.

By the cynic, the sad, the fallen, who had no strength for the strife,

The world's highway is cumbered to day; they make up the sum of life.

But the virtue that conquers passion, and the sorrow that hides in a smile,

It is these that are worth the homage on earth

For we find them but once in a while.

Ella Wheeler Wilcox (1850-1919) started writing poetry at an early age and became famous even before she graduated high school. She was paid $5 by the New York Sun for her first published poem in 1883.

FEAR NOT

#10

GOD'S ANSWER

"Fear God, yes, but don't be afraid of Him."

J. A. Spender

Cheerful Heart

Joel 2:1-21 (NIV)

"Even now," declares the Lord, "return to me with all your heart, with fasting, weeping and mourning."

Rend your heart and not your garments.

Return to the Lord your God, for he is gracious and compassionate,

Slow to anger and abounding in love, and he relents from sending calamity.

Who knows? He may turn and have pity and leave behind a blessing—

Grain offering and drink offerings for the Lord your God.

Blow the trumpet in Zion, declare a holy fast, call a sacred assembly.

Gather the people, consecrate the assembly; bring together the elders,

Gather the children, those nursing at the breast.

Let the bridegroom leave his room and the bride her chamber.

Let the priests, who minister before the Lord, weep between the temple porch and the altar.

Let them say, "Spare your people, O Lord.

Do not make your inheritance an object of scorn, a byword among the nations.

Why should they say among the peoples, 'Where is their God?'"

Then the Lord will be jealous for his land and take pity on his people.

The Lord will reply to them:

"I am sending you grain, new wine and oil, enough to satisfy you fully;

Never again will I make you an object of scorn to the nations.

Be not afraid*, O land; be glad and rejoice." Surely the Lord has done great things.*

"A cheerful heart is good medicine." *Proverbs 17:22.*

God's Answer

***FEAR NOT, O Land; be glad and rejoice: for the Lord will do great things.* Joel 2:21 (KJV)**

We had to get up quite early to make it to a distant hospital in time for my second surgery. Before we left the house, Jack wanted to take a picture of me with the children.

I asked him, "Do you think I'm going to die?" No, he just wanted a before and after picture.

We got halfway there and I remembered that I forgot to pack my favorite "Elmo" stuffed animal. Laurie and Delano gave him to me and I always take him to the hospital. My dear husband said, "Don't worry, I packed him for you." What a guy, huh?

As we went over the high mountain pass, I began to think about all of the people who were praying at that very moment for me and the upcoming surgery.

Suddenly, I just *felt* the prayers of those people. I have never experienced anything like it before or since. Any fear that I had completely vanished. I felt peace. I felt joy. It really is very hard to explain.

But I knew that I felt it.

Prayer does change things.

I like to tell the grandkids that God *always* answers prayer. Sometimes He says, "Yes," sometimes He says "No," and sometimes He says "Wait." I had waited a long time for this surgery, eighteen years in fact. And now He was saying "Yes."

What great thing was God going to do in my life during the next week? I would be gone from home and family. I would be suffering. But I would not be alone for He is always with me. **"His rod and His staff, they comfort me."** Psalm 23 (KJV)

Comfort.

That's the main thing I felt when I felt the prayers of the people. May God give you His comfort today as you go through what you are going through. And please know that my prayers are with you too.

Joel 2:21

BE NOT AFRAID, O land; be glad and rejoice. Surely the Lord has done great things. (NIV)

A Bag of Tools

Isn't it strange

That princes and kings,

And clowns that caper

In sawdust rings,

And common people

Like you and me

Are builders for eternity?

Each is given a bag of tools,

A shapeless mass,

A book of rules;

And each must make—

Ere life is flown—

A stumbling block

Or a steppingstone.

R. L. Sharpe

FEAR NOT

#9

A BLESSING

"You gain strength, courage and confidence

by every experience in which you really stop to look fear in the face.

You are able to say to yourself,

'I have lived through this horror; I can take the next thing that comes along.'

You must do the thing you think you cannot do."

Eleanor Roosevelt

Commandments

Zechariah 8:3-17 (NKJV)

Thus says the Lord: "I will return to Zion, and dwell in the midst of Jerusalem. Jerusalem shall be called the City of Truth, the Mountain of the Lord of Hosts, the Holy Mountain."

Thus says the Lord of Hosts: "Old men and old women shall again sit in the streets of Jerusalem, each one with his staff in his hand because of great age. The streets of the city shall be full of boys and girls playing in its streets."

Thus says the Lord of Hosts: "Let your hands be strong, you who have been hearing in these days these words by the mouth of the prophets, who spoke in the day the foundation was laid for the house of the Lord of Hosts, that the temple might be built.

"For before these days there were no wages for man nor any hire for beast; there was no peace from the enemy for whoever went out or came in; for I set all men, everyone, against his neighbor. But now I will not treat the remnant of this people as in the former days," says the Lord of Hosts.

"For the seed shall be prosperous, the vine shall give its fruit, the ground shall give her increase, and the heavens shall give their dew—I will cause the remnant of this people to possess all these. And it shall come to pass that just as you were a curse among the nations, O house of Judah and house of Israel, so I will save you, and you shall be a blessing.

*"**Do not fear**, let your hands be strong."*

For thus says the Lord of Hosts: "Just as I determined to punish you when your fathers provoked me to wrath, and I would not relent, so again in these days I am determined to do good to Jerusalem and to the house of Judah.

Do not fear.

These are the things you shall do:

"Speak each man the truth to his neighbor; give judgment in your gates for truth, justice, and peace; let none of you think evil in your heart against your neighbor; and do not love a false oath. For all these are things that I hate," says the Lord.

For the story of the stone tablets given to Moses on Mt. Sinai, please read Exodus 20.

A Blessing

And it shall come to pass, that as ye were a curse among the heathen, O house of Judah, and house of Israel; so will I save you, and ye shall be a blessing: FEAR NOT, but let your hands be strong.
Zechariah 8:13 (KJV)

Well, it was time to say a final goodbye—maybe I'll see you later—to my family and pastor. They wheeled me into Pre-Op and dropped the bomb.

"We will not be able to do this surgery unless you let us intubate you *before* we put you to sleep. We'll give you half an hour to decide."

Oh, no! I wanted my family!

Why didn't they tell me this weeks ago so that I could have studied out all of the pros and cons?

Here I am all alone, with my family just down the hall and I have to make a decision like this? I wanted to ask to see my family, but I didn't.

And then I realized that of course I wasn't alone.

God was still with me and He was the best choice after all. So, we worked through it and when the half hour was up, I gave them my answer.

As I lay in the operating room and they began the procedure, I felt the many hands that held my arms down so that I wouldn't flail. I felt the many hands that held my legs down so that I wouldn't kick. I saw the many pairs of eyes that looked down on me with pity.

But, once again, I was perfectly calm.

I didn't even move a finger because I knew it would only make it worse for everyone.

It wasn't me, though, it was God. I was amazed to discover that He was there again, just when I needed Him the most.

What a miracle. What a blessing!

Zechariah 8:13

And it shall come to pass, that as ye were a curse among the heathen, O house of Judah, and house of Israel; so will I save you, and ye shall be a blessing: FEAR NOT, but let your hands be strong. (NIV)

Blessed Be the Name of the Lord

O for a thousand tongues to sing my great Redeemer's praise,

The glories of my God and King, the triumphs of His grace.

My gracious Master and my God, assist me to proclaim,

To spread through all the earth abroad the honors of Thy name.

Jesus, the name that charms our fears, that bids our sorrows cease;

'Tis music in the sinner's ears, 'tis life, and health, and peace.

He beaks the power of canceled sin, he sets the prisoner free;

His blood can make the foulest clean; His blood availed for me.

Hear Him, ye deaf; His praise, ye dumb, your loosened tongues employ;

Ye blind, behold your Savior comes; and leap ye lame for joy.

Blessed be the name,
Blessed be the name,
Blessed be the name of the Lord.
Blessed be the name,
Blessed be the name,
Blessed be the name of the Lord.

Charles Wesley (1707-1788) and his brother, John (1703-1791), were among the first traveling evangelists in England. Born in Lincolnshire, they were the leaders of the Methodist Movement along with George Whitefield. For a short time, Charles was the chaplain at Fort Frederica on St. Simon's Island in Georgia before the Revolutionary War, but he is best known for the many hymns he wrote and arranged—over 6,000.

FEAR NOT

#8

JUDGMENT DAY

"The greatest mistake you can make in life is to be continually fearing you will make one."

Elbert Hubbard

Judah & Jerusalem

Malachi 2:17 & 3:1-7 (NIV)

You have wearied the Lord with your words.

"How have we wearied Him?" you ask.

By saying, "All who do evil are good in the eyes of the Lord,

and He is pleased with them" or "Where is the God of justice?"

"See, I will send my messenger, who will prepare the way before me.

Then suddenly the Lord you are seeking will come to His temple;

the messenger of the covenant, whom you desire, will come," says the Lord Almighty.

"But who can endure the day of His coming? Who can stand when He appears?

For He will be like a refiner's fire or a launderer's soap.

He will sit as a refiner and purifier of silver; He will purify the Levites and refine them like gold and silver.

Then the Lord will have men who will bring offerings in righteousness,

and the offerings of Judah and Jerusalem will be acceptable to the Lord,

as in days gone by, as in former years.

"So I will come near to you for judgment.

I will be quick to testify against sorcerers, adulterers and perjurers,

against those who defraud laborers of their wages, who oppress the widows and the fatherless,

and deprive aliens of justice,

***Do not fear** me," says the Lord Almighty.*

"I the Lord do not change.

So you, O descendants of Jacob, are not destroyed.

Ever since the time of your forefathers you have turned away from my decrees and have not kept them.

Return to me, and I will return to you," says the Lord Almighty.

For the story of Jacob, please read Genesis Chapter 27.

Judgment Day

"And FEAR NOT me," saith the Lord of Hosts. For I am the Lord, I change not; therefore ye sons of Jacob are not consumed." Malachi 3:5 & 6 (KJV)

All sin is the same to God. Sin is sin. Man is the one who has categorized sin. I remember the first time I heard a sermon to that affect and it profoundly shocked me. I was prideful because I had never committed murder or adultery or practiced sorcery.

However, God does talk about abominations. He says in Proverbs 12:22 that:

"Lying lips are an abomination to the Lord."

Oops, I've told some lies in my time, haven't you? Well, maybe they were only "little white lies." No, a lie is a lie is a lie.

My sister and I had baby boys only two months apart and then thirteen months later, she had a baby girl. Everywhere we went, everyone thought that the boys were twins and it didn't help that my Mom always bought them matching outfits. One time, the whole kitchen crew in a Chinese restaurant came to our table to "see the twins."

As you can imagine, it was necessary to explain that no, they weren't twins, just cousins close in age.

One day I had all three little ones with me at the park. It had been a long day and I was very tired. A lady came by, noticed them playing and asked, "Oh, are they TRIPLETS?" I didn't want to take the time to explain the whole story---

So I just said "yes."

Unsaved people who treat us badly can be saved in an instant. Don't they deserve the same grace we received? I once asked a high school Sunday school class if God could forgive Saddam Hussein?

Half of them said no.

I am so thankful that He will not destroy me because I sin.

There's something that I *don't* have to fear!

Malachi 3:5 & 6

"DO NOT FEAR ME," says the Lord Almighty. "I the Lord do not change. So you, O descendants of Jacob are not destroyed." (NIV)

I Know Something Good About You

Wouldn't this old world be better
If the folks we meet would say—
"I know something good about you!"
And treat us just that way?

Wouldn't it be fine and dandy
If each handclasp, fond and true,
Carried with it this assurance—
"I know something good about you!"

Wouldn't life be lots more happy
If the good that's in us all
Were the only thing about us
That folks bothered to recall?

Wouldn't life be lots more happy
If we praised the good we see?
For there's such a lot of goodness
In the worst of you and me!

Wouldn't it be nice to practice
That fine way of thinking, too?
You know something good about me,
I know something good about you!

Louis C. Shimon

FEAR NOT

#7

BIRTH OF JESUS

"We see things; we think about things;

and we choose our course of action or beliefs, appropriately.

As long as that remains true of us,

we will live every day of our lives on one slippery slope or another.

There is no reason to fear this."

Real Live Preacher

Joseph & Mary

Matthew 1:20-2:12 (NKJV)

Now the birth of Jesus Christ was as follows: After his mother Mary was betrothed to Joseph, before they came together, she was found with child of the Holy Spirit. Then Joseph her husband, being a just man, and not wanting to make her a public example, was minded to put her away secretly.

But while he thought about these things, behold, an angel of the Lord appeared to him in a dream, saying, "Joseph, son of David, **do not be afraid** *to take to you Mary your wife, for that which is conceived in her is of the Holy Spirit. And she shall bring forth a Son, and you shall call His name JESUS, for He will save his people from their sins."*

So all this was done that it might be fulfilled which was spoken by the Lord through the prophet, saying: "Behold, the virgin shall be with child, and bear a son, and they shall call his name Immanuel," which is translated, "God with us" (Isaiah 7:14). Then Joseph, being aroused from sleep, did as the angel of the Lord commanded him and took to him his wife, and did not know her till she had brought forth her firstborn son. And he called His name Jesus.

Now after Jesus was born in Bethlehem of Judea in the days of Herod the king, behold, wise men from the East came to Jerusalem, saying, "Where is He who has been born King of the Jews? For we have seen His star in the East and have come to worship Him." When Herod the king heard this, he was troubled, and all Jerusalem with him. And when he had gathered all the chief priests and scribes of the people together, he inquired of them where the Christ was to be born.

So they said to him, "In Bethlehem of Judea, for thus it is written by the prophet: 'But you, Bethlehem, in the land of Judah, are not the least among the rulers of Judah; for out of you shall come a Ruler who will shepherd my people Israel' (Micah 5:2). Then Herod, when he had secretly called the wise men, determined from them what time the star appeared. And he sent them to Bethlehem and said, "Go and search carefully for the young child, and when you have found him, bring back word to me, that I may come and worship him also."

When they heard the king, they departed; and behold, the star which they had seen in the East went before them, till it came and stood over where the young child was. When they saw the star, they rejoiced with exceedingly great joy. And when they had come into the house, they saw the young child with Mary his mother, and fell down and worshiped him. And when they had opened their treasures, they presented gifts to him: gold, frankincense, and myrrh. Then, being divinely warned in a dream that they should not return to Herod, they departed for their own country another way.

For the story of Christmas, please read Luke 2.

Birth of Jesus

"But while he thought on these things, behold the angel of the Lord appeared unto him in a dream saying, "Joseph, thou son of David, FEAR NOT to take unto thee Mary thy wife: for that which is conceived in her is of the Holy Ghost." Matthew 1:20 (KJV)

I was raised in a Christian home and accepted Jesus as my Savior at an early age during a Kids Crusade at church. I have served Him all of my life. It wasn't until the age of ten that I decided to find out for myself what is was to be a daughter of God. I remember the feeling of conviction I had and I knew I had to go up front no matter who saw me. I'm so glad I did.

When Laurie and Delano were 5 and 3, my Dad was dying of cancer and they wanted to know more about Heaven. I explained that we can go to Heaven if we've asked Jesus into our hearts and they both immediately said that they wanted to do that. I wondered at the time if they were a little too young for it to "stick," but they are both serving the Lord today.

I have also had the privilege of being with my grandchildren when they accepted Jesus into their hearts. It was the night the Strength Team came to our church and all three went forward. I went up with them and we stood there holding hands and crying.

If Jesus had not come and given his life for our sins, I could have experienced none of these things. To this day I have not watched *The Passion of the Christ* (the one done by Mel Gibson) and don't know if I ever can. Our church has a huge wooden cross with a purple robe draped across it in the corner of the sanctuary and I can hardly look at it without tearing up.

If He had not come, who would have been with me all those times before, during and after surgery when I was so scared and felt alone? Each time I cried out to Him, He reminded me that I was not alone and that my fear was simply unbelief. Having believed in Him all of my life, I struggle with my fears—fears that I have every day even when I'm not facing a surgery.

What can I possibly have to fear with Jesus at my side? After going through emotional, financial or physical need, I can always look back and see that He carried me through it all and worked it out His way, the perfect way. I see this over and over again in my life and still I fear.

Matthew 1:20

"But after he had considered this, an angel of the Lord appeared to him in a dream and said, "Joseph son of David, DO NOT BE AFRAID to take Mary home as your wife, because what is conceived in her is from the Holy Spirit."(NIV)

Joy to the World!

Joy to the world, the Lord is come; let earth receive her King;

Let every heart prepare Him room, and Heaven and nature sing,

And Heaven and nature sing, and Heaven, and Heaven and nature sing.

Joy to the earth, the Savior reigns; let men their songs employ;

While fields and floods, rocks, hills, and plains, repeat the sounding joy,

Repeat the sounding joy, repeat, repeat the sounding joy.

No more let sins and sorrows grow, nor thorns infest the ground;

He comes to make His blessings flow far as the curse if found,

Far as the curse is found, far as, far as the curse is found.

He rules the world with truth and grace, and makes the nations prove

The glories of His righteousness, and wonders of His love,

And wonders of His love, and wonders, and wonders of His love.

Isaac Watts (1674-1748) was known as the "Father of English Hymns" and also formed many of David's Psalms into music for the church. He was also an author and one of his books on logic had an extraordinary title: *Logic; or the Right Use of Reason in the Enquiry After Truth With a Variety of Rules to Guard Against Error in the Affairs of Religion and Human Life as Well as in the Sciences*! What a mouthful!

FEAR NOT

#6

KILL THE BODY

"The fear of the Lord is the beginning of wisdom,

and knowledge of the Holy One is understanding." Proverbs 9:10

King Solomon

Jesus & Disciples

Matthew 10:3-28 (NKJV)

These twelve Jesus sent out and commanded them, saying: "Do not go into the way of the Gentiles, and do not enter a city of the Samaritans. But go rather to the lost sheep of the house of Israel. And as you go, preach, saying, 'The kingdom of heaven is at hand.' Heal the sick, cleanse the lepers, raise the dead, cast out demons. Freely you have received, freely give. Provide neither gold nor silver nor copper in your money belts, nor bag for your journey, nor two tunics, nor sandals, nor staffs; for a worker is worthy of his food.

"Now whatever city or town you enter, enquire who in it is worthy, and stay there till you go out. And when you go into a household, greet it. If the household is worthy, let your peace come upon it. But if it is not worthy, let your peace return to you. And whoever will not receive you nor hear your words, when you depart from that house or city, shake off the dust from your feet. Assuredly, I say to you, it will be more tolerable for the land of Sodom and Gomorrah in the day of judgment than for that city!

"Behold, I send you out as sheep in the midst of wolves. Therefore be wise as serpents and harmless as doves. But beware of men, for they will deliver you up to councils and scourge you in their synagogues. You will be brought before governors and kings for my sake, as a testimony to them and to the Gentiles. But when they deliver you up, do not worry about how or what you should speak. For it will be given to you in that hour what you should speak; for it is not you who speak, but the Spirit of your father who speaks in you.

"Now brother will deliver up brother to death, and a father his child; and children will rise up against parents and cause them to be put to death. And you will be hated by all for my name's sake. But he who endures to the end will be saved. When they persecute you in this city, flee to another. For assuredly, I say to you, you will not have gone through the cities of Israel before the Son of Man comes.

*"A disciple is not above his teacher, nor a servant above his master. It is enough for a disciple that he be like his teacher, and a servant like his master. If they have called the master of the house Beelzebub, how much more will they call those of his household! Therefore **do not fear** them. For there is nothing covered that will not be revealed, and hidden that will not be known.*

*"Whatever I tell you in the dark, speak in the light; and what you hear in the ear, preach on the housetops. And **do not fear** those who kill the body but cannot kill the soul. But rather fear him who is able to destroy both soul and body in hell."*

For the Great Commission that Jesus gave to all Christians, please read Matthew 28:16.

Kill the Body

"FEAR NOT them which kill the body, but are not able to kill the soul: but rather fear him which is able to destroy both soul and body in hell." **Matthew 10:28 (KJV)**

When Laurie and Delano were preschoolers, I became seriously ill. I was so sick that I just lay on the couch all day long. It was all I could do to get up and make it to the bathroom. Laurie would get their cereal every morning and make peanut butter and jelly sandwiches for them at lunchtime. When Jack came home after work he had to cook dinner, bathe the kids, do the laundry and clean the house.

I began to realize that I was dying.

Soon after this, my Dad found out that he had cancer. He got worse and worse. One time I got up in the middle of the night to go to the bathroom and I looked across the street to where my parents lived. I saw a light on and knew that my mother was up with him. As clear as a bell, I heard a voice say inside, "I'm going to take him instead of you."

Immediately the words to a poem flooded my brain and I wrote them down:

> *"I held my Daddy's hand when I was very small.*
> *It always seemed so big to me and he so very tall.*
> *We did so many happy things together, side by side,*
> *And as I grew, I came to know a special daughterly pride.*
> *The memories, oh, so special, are very clear to me.*
> *The things we did—the time spent—we were a family.*
> *And then my Daddy's hand began to shrink and fade away.*
> *He died and went to Heaven one sad and mournful day.*
> *I'll hold my Daddy's hand again I know with all my heart.*
> *It'll be strong and big again, and up there we'll never part."*

Two months later he was gone and I began to get well.

Life is so short and just as Jesus instructed His disciples to preach this message: **"The kingdom of Heaven is near,"** so should we as Christians witness to every one we meet. I used to think that was a job for only pastors and missionaries, but now I know that it means me also. Sometimes preaching a message of God's love is a simple as doing a right instead of a wrong, treating people with respect and greeting everyone with a smile.

Matthew 10:28

"DO NOT BE AFRAID of those who kill the body but cannot kill the soul. Rather, BE AFRAID of the One who can destroy both soul and body in hell." **(NIV)**

The Old Rugged Cross

On a hill far away stood an old rugged cross, the emblem of suffering and shame;

And I love that old cross where the dearest and best for a world of lost sinners was slain.

Oh, the old rugged cross, so despised by the world, has a wondrous attraction for me;

For the dear Lamb of God left His glory above to bear it to dark Calvary.

In the old rugged cross, stained with blood so divine, a wondrous beauty I see;

For 'twas on that old cross Jesus suffered and died to pardon and sanctify me.

To the old rugged cross I will ever be true, its shame and reproach gladly bear;

Then He'll call me some day to my home far away, where His glory forever I'll share.

So I'll cherish the old rugged cross,
Till my trophies at last I lay down;
I will cling to the old rugged cross,
And exchange it some day for a crown.

Reverend George Bennard (1873-1958) always wanted a career as an evangelist, but after his father died, he went to work to support his mother and sisters. Later, he and his wife worked for the Salvation Army. He spent the last years of his life in Reed City, Michigan and it is there that you can visit the Old Rugged Cross Historical Museum. I remember this song from the first funeral I ever went to, at the age of ten, when my father's father died.

FEAR NOT

#5

WORTH MORE

"You see what power is—holding someone else's fear in your hand and showing it to them!"

Amy Tan

Sparrows

Matthew 10:29-42 (NIV)

"Are not two sparrows sold for a penny?

Yet not one of these will fall to the ground apart from the will of your Father.

And even the very hairs of your head are all numbered.

Don't be afraid; *you are worth more than many sparrows.*

Whoever acknowledges me before men, I will also acknowledge him before my Father in heaven.

But whoever disowns me before men, I will disown him before my Father in heaven.

Do not suppose that I have come to bring peace to the earth.

I did not come to bring peace, but a sword.

'For I have come to turn a man against his father, a daughter against her mother,

a daughter-in-law against her mother-in-law—

a man's enemies will be the members of his own household.' (Micah 7:6)

Anyone who loves his father or mother more than me is not worthy of me;

anyone who loves his son or daughter more than me is not worthy of me;

and anyone who does not take his cross and follow me is not worthy of me.

Whoever finds his life will lose it, and whoever loses his life for my sake will find it.

He who receives you receives me, and he who receives me receives the one who sent me.

Anyone who receives a prophet because he is a prophet will receive a prophet's reward,

and anyone who receives a righteous man because he is a righteous man

will receive a righteous man's reward.

And if anyone gives even a cup of cold water to one of these little ones because he is my disciple,

I tell you the truth, he will certainly not lose his reward."

For encouragement in not worrying, please read Matthew 6:25-34.

Sparrows

***"FEAR YE NOT therefore, ye are of more value than many sparrows."* Matthew 10:31 (KJV)**

When I was a young girl, I overheard my mother talking with a friend. The friend's daughter had grown up in the church and was a Christian, but she fell in love with an unsaved man. She married him anyway and was confident that she could get him to attend church and become a Christian. He never did get saved and they had a terrible marriage that ended in a bitter divorce.

I vowed that I would never do that.

During my senior year in high school, a young man asked me out. He wasn't a believer, but I figured that a few dates wouldn't hurt. We began to date steadily and soon fell in love. He asked me to marry him and I panicked. I was in love and wanted to marry him, but I just couldn't let myself do that because he wasn't a Christian. That old story kept going around and around in my head. So, I put him off. I couldn't tell him the real reason because I didn't want him to say he was a Christian just so I would marry him.

The summer after my graduation, I went to Europe on a foreign study program. He wanted to give me an engagement ring before I left, but I wouldn't accept it. While I was gone, my brother kept taking him to church and blessedly, he got saved. When I returned home, he told me the news and asked me to marry him again. I was so relieved, and this time I was able to say yes.

And then I told him the story that I overheard. We will be married 39 years this October.

This is the guy who remembered to pack my stuffed Elmo when we went to the big city for one of my surgeries. This is the guy who took care of me at the hospital and at home each time I had surgery. This is the guy who worked extra long hours on the farm so that I wouldn't have to get a job and could homeschool our two children. This is the guy that I thought I loved more than God. Sorry, honey, I now know that I love God more, but that's the way it's supposed to be.

Anyway, he was the best nurse I ever had and tried to do more for me than necessary. I often reminded him to let me do it myself, so that I could gain my strength back.

When you're in the hospital, it seems like you go days without a shower and that first one is such a pleasure. I remember when the nurse said that I could have one and Jack volunteered to do it for her.

This is the guy who washed my hair when I could barely sit up.

Matthew 10:31

***"So DON'T BE AFRAID; you are worth more than many sparrows."* (NIV)**

His Eye is on the Sparrow

Why should I feel discouraged, why should the shadows come,
Why should my heart be lonely and long for Heaven and Home,
When Jesus is my portion? My constant Friend is He.
His eye is on the sparrow and I know He watches me.

"Let not your heart be troubled," His tender words I hear,
And resting on His goodness, I lose my doubts and fears;
Though by the path He leads me, but one step I may see;
His eye is on the sparrow and I know He watches me.

Whenever I am tempted, whenever clouds arise,
When songs give place to sighing, when hope within me dies,
I draw the closer to Him, from care He sets me free.
His eye is on the sparrow and I know He watches me.

I sing because I'm happy,
I sing because I'm free,
For His eye is on the sparrow,
And I know He watches me.

Civila Durfee Martin (1866-1948) was born in Nova Scotia, Canada and married Walter Stillman Martin who put music to her poems. Together they authored several hundred hymns. The inspiration for this song was from the Bible verse in Matthew as well as Mr. and Mrs. Doolittle—she was bedridden for over 20 years and he was in a wheelchair. When asked how she kept up her spirits, Mrs. Doolittle said, "His eye is on the sparrow and I know He watches me."

FEAR NOT

#4

BACK TO LIFE

"To fear the foe, since fear oppresseth strength, gives in your weakness strength unto your foe."

William Shakespeare

Jairus & Daughter

Luke 8:40-56 (NKJV)

So it was, when Jesus returned, that the multitude welcomed Him, for they were all waiting for Him. And behold, there came a man named Jairus, and he was a ruler of the synagogue. He fell down at Jesus' feet and begged Him to come to his house, for he had an only daughter about twelve years of age, and she was dying.

But as He went, the multitudes thronged Him. Now a woman, having a flow of blood for twelve years, who had spent all her livelihood on physicians and could not be healed by any, came from behind and touched the border of His garment. And immediately her flow of blood stopped.

And Jesus said, "Who touched me?"

When all denied it, Peter and those with him said, "Master, the multitudes throng and press you, and you say, 'Who touched me?'"

But Jesus said, "Somebody touched me, for I perceived power going out from me."

Now when the woman saw that she was not hidden, she came trembling; and falling down before Him, she declared to Him in the presence of all the people the reason she had touched Him and how she was healed immediately.

And he said to her, "Daughter, be of good cheer; your faith has made you well. Go in peace."

While He was still speaking, someone came from the ruler of the synagogue's house, saying to him, "Your daughter is dead. Do not trouble the teacher."

*But when Jesus heard it, He answered him saying, "**Do not be afraid**; only believe, and she will be made well."*

When He came into the house, He permitted no one to go in except Peter, James, and John, and the father and mother of the girl.

Now all wept and mourned for her; but He said, "Do not weep; she is not dead, but sleeping."

And they ridiculed Him, knowing that she was dead. But He put them all outside, took her by the hand and called, saying, "Little girl, arise."

Then her spirit returned, and she arose immediately. And He commanded that she be given something to eat. And her parents were astonished, but He charged them to tell no one what had happened.

For the story of a boy who was healed, please read Luke 7:11-17.

Back to Life

"But when Jesus heard it, he answered him, saying, 'FEAR NOT: believe only, and she shall be made whole.'" Luke 8:50 (KJV)

I just love it when the Bible speaks specifically to a situation in my life. I did not lose a child, but I did have an issue of blood—not for twelve years though. Today we just have an operation and it is taken care of. Imagine how awful it would have been all those years ago. It's a miracle in itself that she never died of anemia.

But, knowing there is an operation stops us from trusting in God to take care of the problem. I heard a preacher say one time, "It's okay to go to the doctor, if you give God the opportunity to heal you first." Sometimes we use prayer as a last resort instead of a first choice.

After my surgery in the big city to have my thyroid removed, I was resting in my hospital bed, completely at peace. Suddenly I saw a bright light at the end of a tunnel and the light kept moving closer and getting bigger. Now, I have heard lots of stories of after death experiences and thought, "Here I come, Lord."

Just as I pressed the call button, I went into convulsions.

The young nurse who burst into my room took one look and her eyes got huge. She tried to inject something into my flailing arms, but finally gave up. At last she popped an antacid into my mouth and the convulsion reduced by half, giving her the opportunity to draw some blood. Did you know that most antacids contain calcium?

Soon the room was full of interns and doctors and they explained that I had gone into calcium shock. I think I told them that I thought I was going to Heaven. This all happened in the middle of the night, of course, and there I was without my family again. But—and you know what I'm going to say—God was right there with me.

In fact, I thought I was going to meet Him face to face.

Have you ever gone into shock? Strange sensation--and afterwards there is this huge urge to use the bathroom! The reason for this is that the fluids in your extremities pool in your core (hence the flailing of the limbs) to save your vital organs and when it's over, those fluids have to go somewhere.

The next day the doctor told me that he thought there was a very good chance that this was going to happen in my case, but he didn't want to mention it as he thought it would make me worry. There's that word *"worry"* again. I suppose I'm glad I didn't have a clue.

Luke 8:50

"Hearing this, Jesus said to Jairus,'DON'T BE AFRAID; just believe, and she will be healed.'" (NIV)

Smile

Like a bread without the spreadin',
Like a puddin' without sauce,
Like a mattress without beddin',
Like a cart without a hoss,
Like a door without a latchstring,
Like a fence without a stile,
Like a dry an' barren creek bed—
Is the face without a smile.

Like a house without a dooryard,
Like a yard without a flower,
Like a clock without a mainspring,
That will never tell the hour;
A thing that sort o' makes yo' feel
A hunger all the while—
Oh, the saddest sight that ever was
Is a face without a smile!

The face of man was built for smiles,
An' thereby he is blest
Above the critters of the field,
The birds an' all the rest;
He's just a little lower
Than the angels in the skies,
An' the reason is that he can smile;
Therein his glory lies!

So smile an' don't forgit to smile,
An' smile, an' smile ag'in;
'Twill help you all along the way,
An' cheer you mile by mile;
An' so, whatever is your lot,
Jes' smile, an' smile, an' smile.

Author Unknown

FEAR NOT

#3

FEAR GOD

"For God did not give us a spirit of fear,

but a spirit of power, of love and of self-discipline." 2 Timothy 1:7

Timothy

Spirit of Fear

Luke 12:1-17 (NIV)

Meanwhile, when a crowd of many thousands had gathered, so that they were trampling on one another, Jesus began to speak first to his disciples, saying:

"Be on your guard against the yeast of the Pharisees, which is hypocrisy. There is nothing concealed that will not be disclosed, or hidden that will not be made known. What you have said in the dark will be heard in the daylight, and what you have whispered in the ear in the inner rooms will be proclaimed from the roofs.

"I tell you, my friends,

Do not be afraid *of those who kill the body and after that can do no more. But I will show you whom you should fear:*

Fear Him *who, after the killing of the body, has power to throw you into hell.*

Yes, I tell, you **fear Him**.

"Are not five sparrows sold for two pennies? Yet not one of them is forgotten by God. Indeed, the very hairs of your head are all numbered.

Don't be afraid; *you are worth more than many sparrows.*

"I tell you, whoever acknowledges me before men, the Son of Man will also acknowledge him before the angels of God.

But he who disowns me before men will be disowned before the angels of God.

And everyone who speaks a word against the Son of Man will be forgiven, but anyone who blasphemes against the Holy Spirit will not be forgiven.

"When you are brought before synagogues, rulers and authorities, do not worry about how you will defend yourselves or what you will say, for the Holy Spirit will teach you at that time what you should say."

For the story of Mary anointing Jesus with perfume, please read John 12:1-11.

Hairs of Your Head

"But even the very hairs of your head are all numbered. FEAR NOT therefore: ye are of more value than many sparrows." Luke 12:7 (KJV)

Have you ever slapped a doctor? I did once. After abdominal surgery, they cautioned me to **never**, and I mean **never**, try get up out of bed without assistance. A few nights passed in which I woke Jack several times to help me, as directed. Finally, on the third night, I decided that I would be fine on my own. I rolled over, stood up and gasped right out loud.

It felt like my incision had burst open and all my intestines had fallen out.

I reached down, but everything was still in one piece, but boy, was I sore. A few days later, we decided that I needed to see a doctor—the pain was getting worse.

The doctor said that I had probably just pulled a stitch and began pushing down on the incision to find the sore spot. Unbelievably, it didn't hurt at all while he was pushing *until* he found the torn spot. Jack said that my body literally lifted up off of the examining table—he saw space under my body. And that's when I did it.

I slapped the doctor's hand and pushed it away. I did not consciously think to do this, it just happened without my will. It hurt so bad, it was a natural reaction from my body to stop the pain. He just grinned, looked at Jack and said, "Well, I guess we found the sore spot!"

I began apologizing profusely and still can't believe that I did that! Looking through my journal entries from that time, I saw a comment I made that will help you understand how sore I was. This is what I wrote, "Sneezed today—oh no!" Imagine being conscious of a little old sneeze. But torn flesh is torn flesh and if you've ever had it happen to you, you know what I mean.

Imagine how our Lord suffered with His extremely bruised and broken body.

I heard one preacher speculate that His back was so lacerated by the whipping that the bones of His ribs were showing through the tatters of skin. His loss of blood is probably why He stumbled and the cross was given to Simon to carry. Remembering the pain that one small torn spot caused me, I can't even begin to imagine how He handled the pain inflicted on Him during that terrible day.

Luke 12:7

"Indeed, the very hairs of your head are all numbered. DON'T BE AFRAID; you are worth more than many sparrows." **(NIV)**

Myself

I have to live with myself, and so
I want to be fit for myself to know,
I want to be able, as days go by,
Always to look myself straight in the eye;
I don't want to stand, with the setting sun,
And hate myself for things I have done.

I don't want to keep on a closet shelf
A lot of secrets about myself,
And fool myself, as I come and go,
Into thinking that nobody else will know
The kind of a man I really am;
I don't want to dress up myself in sham.

I want to go out with my head erect,
I want to deserve all men's respect;
But here in the struggle for fame and self
I want to be able to like myself.
I don't want to look at myself and know
That I'm bluster and bluff and empty show.

I can never hide myself from me;
I see what others may never see;
I know what others may never know,
I never can fool myself, and so,
Whatever happens, I want to be
Self-respecting and conscience free.

Edgar Albert Guest (1881-1959) was known as the *People's Poet* after he immigrated to America from England. He started as a copy boy at *Detroit Free Press* and was a reporter when his first poem was printed at the age of 17. During his lifetime he wrote over 11,000 cheerful poems that were syndicated in over 300 newspapers and compiled into 20 books.

FEAR NOT

#2

ABOUT LIFE

"He has not learned the lesson of life who does not every day surmount a fear."

Ralph Waldo Emerson

Do Not Worry

Luke 12:22-34 (NKJV)

Then he said to his disciples,

"Therefore I say to you, do not worry about your life, what you will eat;

nor about the body, what you will put on.

Life is more than food, and the body is more than clothing.

Consider the ravens, for they neither sow nor reap,

which have neither storehouse nor barn; and God feeds them.

O how much more value are you than the birds? And which of you by worrying can add one cubit to his stature? If you then are not able to do the least, why are you anxious for the rest?

Consider the lilies, how they grow: they neither toil nor spin; and yet I say to you, even Solomon in all his glory was not arrayed like one of these.

If then God so clothes the grass, which today is in the field and tomorrow is thrown into the oven, how much more will he clothe you, O you of little faith?

And do not seek what you should eat or what you should drink, nor have an anxious mind.

For all these things the nations of the world seek after, and your Father knows that you need these things.

But seek the kingdom of God, and all these things shall be added to you.

***Do not fear**, little flock, for it is your Father's good pleasure to give you the kingdom.*

Sell what you have and give alms.

Provide yourselves money bags which do not grow old, a treasure in the heavens that does not fail.

Where no thief approaches nor moth destroys.

For where your treasure is, there your heart will be also."

For the story of Solomon's great splendor, please read 1 Kings 10:14-29.

Don't Worry

"FEAR NOT, little flock; for it is your Father's good pleasure to give you the kingdom." Luke 12:32 (KJV)

The thing I worry about most is waiting for the results of a cancer biopsy. One day you convince yourself that it can only be good news and the next day you feel you are probably going to die. Maybe I struggle with this so much because my Dad actually died of cancer. Also because I've had lots of biopsies.

There is no other fear quite like it. For example, fear of financial ruin can be remedied by getting a second or higher paying job and cutting back on expenses. Fear for the salvation of your children and grandchildren can be remedied by taking every opportunity to lead them to the Lord. Fear of the dark can be remedied by forcing yourself to conquer that fear.

But a biopsy is either good or bad and there's nothing you can do to change it. I remember the day my doctor told me that I had melanoma and would have to have more surgery. It was like a dream that wasn't true. To this day, I still think they made a mistake.

My daughter was in the room with me and all I could think about was that I had to go to the bathroom. I excused myself and left knowing that everyone probably thought I only wanted to go in there to cry. But I didn't cry and I wasn't afraid--*at first*.

Because I had a lot of moles, we decided to remove them just to guard against any further problems with skin cancer. Waiting for those biopsies was very different from the first time. It's also hard for me to wait for the results of a mammogram.

When I went in for my hysterectomy, the anesthesiologist came in and as he was setting up my IV, he asked me an unbelievable question. He said, "Would you like to be put to sleep or do you want to remain awake during the surgery with only a spinal block?"

Stunned, I answered, "Please, put me to sleep!" and thought, "Why would I want to be awake for something like that?" I have since met people who want to remain alert and hear all the details in the operating room. Not me. Not ever. In fact, I wish there was a way to sleep until the results of my biopsies come back.

Or I could just pray and ask God to take away my worries.

Luke 12:32

"DO NOT BE AFRAID, little flock, for your Father has been pleased to give you the kingdom." (NIV)

Concord Hymn

By the rude bridge that arched the flood,
Their flag to April's breezes unfurled,
Here once the embattled farmers stood,
And fired the shot heard round the world.

The foe long since in silence slept;
Alike the conqueror silent sleeps;
And time the ruined bridge has swept
Down the dark stream which seaward creeps.

On this green bank, by this soft stream,
We set to-day a votive stone;
That memory may their deed redeem,
When, like our sires, our sons are gone.

Spirit, that made those spirits dare,
To die, and leave their children free,
Bid Time and Nature gently spare
The shaft we raise to Them and Thee.

Ralph Waldo Emerson (1803-1882) wrote this poem to commemorate the militiamen who engaged in the war that made us a free country. Written in 1836 for the dedication of the Obelisk in Concord, Massachusetts, he lived less than one hundred paces from where the battle on the Cambridge Concord Turnpike took place. *"The shot heard round the world"* was the most famous line he ever penned.

FEAR NOT

#1

HOME!

"Does Job fear God for nothing?" Satan replied.

"Have you not put a hedge around him and his household and everything he has?"

Book of Job

Hosanna!

John 12:12-19 (NKJV)

The next day a great multitude that had come to the feast,

when they heard that Jesus was coming to Jerusalem,

took branches of palm trees and went out to meet him, and cried out:

"Hosanna!" (which means "save").

"Blessed is he who comes in the name of the Lord!" (Psalms 118:25).

"Blessed is the King of Israel!"

Then Jesus, when he had found a young donkey, sat on it; as it is written:

***"Fear not**, daughter of Zion;*

behold your king is coming sitting on a donkey's colt." (Zechariah 9:9).

His disciples did not understand these things at first;

but when Jesus was glorified, then they remembered

that these things were written about Him and that they had done these things to Him.

Therefore the people,

who were with Him when he called Lazarus out of his tomb

and raised him from the dead, bore witness.

For this reason the people also met Him, because they heard that He had done this sign.

The Pharisees therefore said among themselves,

"You see that you are accomplishing nothing. Look, the world has gone after Him!"

For the story of Jesus raising Lazarus from the dead, please read John 11.

Home!

"FEAR NOT, Daughter of Zion and behold thy King cometh, sitting on a donkey's colt." John 12:15 (NIV)

The best thing about a stay in the hospital is coming home to your own bed. The only thing I miss about a hospital bed is that button that adjusts the position of the bed—high or low/sit up or lie down. Have you ever noticed how noisy it is in the hospital? Well, maybe not noisy, but the nurses are so busy coming and going and taking vital signs. Sometimes you just manage to fall asleep and here they come.

But, that is their job and when you need them (like calcium shock!), it is great to have them. Plus, I always liked it when people came to visit me. But one time I was a bit rude (unintentionally) to one of my guests. I always have a hard time getting over the anesthetic (and yet I still want it) and sometimes it takes me a few days to fully wake up. The kids liked to ask me questions and then laugh when it took me about five minutes to formulate an answer.

Anyway, on this particular day, a cousin and her husband had stopped by in the afternoon to see how I was doing. I really did try to concentrate on what she was saying, but I noticed myself dropping off every few minutes. She was very understanding, having gone through several surgeries herself.

Another nice thing is eating your own (or someone else's) home cooking. Our church is always very good about providing meals for the first week or so. And then my son took over the cooking, so I was very blessed.

I remember one time in the hospital when I had just had my thyroid out and my throat was very, very sore. I mean it was very, very sore on day three. Day one and day two were indescribable. I was only three years old when I had my tonsils out and the nurse told me I had to eat something or I couldn't go home. Mom said I swallowed that jello with many a grimace, but I wanted out of there!

This time it amused me to see what they brought me to eat. One day it was a plate full of chewy rib meat with a spicy hot sauce. That would sure feel good on a raw throat, don't you think? I passed the plate right on to Jack. Once again I was told that I had to eat something or I couldn't go home. Jack said I swallowed that canned pear with many a grimace, but I wanted out of there!

WELCOME HOME!

John 12:15

"DO NOT BE AFRAID, O Daughter of Zion; see, your king is coming, seated on a donkey's colt." (NIV)

Sojourn

I'm a sojourner here; this is not my destination.

I'm headed for a place that will exceed all expectation.

My journey may be long, with a detour, maybe two.

But I'll keep traveling on, until Heaven comes in view.

My treasures are laid up in Heaven, quite secure.

There's nothing on this earth that holds any allure.

You can't take it with you, the silver, nor the gold.

I don't know why you'd want to, Heaven's riches are untold.

All I can take with me is my family.

I want them all to go, so we can spend eternity

Together with the Savior, walking hand in hand.

My journey will have ended when I reach that Promised Land.

Melissa Phillips Wolf and her husband Denny reside in Jenkins, Missouri with their two children, Kiley and Connor. She enjoys living in a rural community surrounded by the beauty of the Ozarks. Melissa has been actively involved in her church for many years, serving as Sunday School teacher, pianist, vocalist, VBS and Christmas Pageant Director, and working with the youth (she's also my cousin!).

Afterward

Now we have a list of all the things we are *not* to fear. Did you know that there are 80 verses in the Bible with the words **"Fear not"** in them? I think God was trying to give us a message.

In Isaiah, **"Fear not"** is mentioned 11 times.

In Genesis, **"Fear not"** is mentioned 8 times.

In Luke, **"Fear not"** is mentioned 7 times.

In Deuteronomy, **"Fear not"** is mentioned 6 times.

In Jeremiah, **"Fear not"** is mentioned 6 times.

Is there really anything we should fear? Yes, God.

Remember what J.A. Spender said in quote #28.

"Fear God, yes, but don't be afraid of Him."

Revelation 14:7 says: ***"Fear God and give glory to Him."***

In this case "fear" doesn't mean to "be afraid," but to respect, honor and revere.

In Psalms, **"Fear God"** is mentioned 41 times.

In Deuteronomy, **"Fear God"** is mentioned 19 times.

In Proverbs, **"Fear God"** is mentioned 17 times.

In Isaiah, **"Fear God"** is mentioned 12 times.

In Job, **"Fear God"** is mentioned 7 times.

I guess it's time to write another devotional. This time about **"Fear God"**.

God said, "Fear not"

To Hagar and Ishmael in the desert;

To Isaac, alone in the night;

To Jacob as he waited in Canaan;

To Israel at the Red Sea;

To Israel when spies went out;

To Israel when facing the Canaanites;

To Israel at the Jordan River;

To Israel when Moses died;

To Joshua when he fought at Ai;

To Israel fighting five powerful kings;

To Gideon while threshing wheat;

To Gideon as he put out his fleece;

To Israel when in bondage to Babylon;

To Solomon at the death of David;

To Jehoshaphat before a vast army;

To David as he cried to the Lord;

To Solomon when asking for wisdom;

To Isaiah when he met King Ahab;

To Israel when their enemies raged;

To Israel when their enemies pursued;

To Israel during their captivity;

To Israel after the Temple was destroyed;

To Israel after God chose them;

To Israel after their salvation with Zion;

To Israel and their future glory;

To Israel and the rebuilding of Judah;

To Israel when Gedaliah was killed;

To Joel after the locusts ate the food;

To Zechariah when the remnant doubted;

To Malachi on Judgment Day;

To Joseph when Mary became pregnant;

To the Disciples when they feared the devil;

To the Disciples when they feared the Samaritans;

To Jairus when they said that his daughter was dead;

To the crowds when they shared their worries;

and

To Israel when Jesus entered Jerusalem, riding on a donkey.

Biographies of Quote People

37. Oprah Gail Winfrey (1945)—Born in Kosciusko, Mississippi to an unwed teenage mother, she was officially named "Orpah" after Naomi's daughter-in-law in the Bible. But since her family didn't know how to pronounce it, she became known as Oprah. She lived with her grandmother for many years and they were so poor she wore dresses made from potato sacks. After being molested, she ran away from home at age 13 and had a baby boy that died a year later. Through the help of the Upward Bound program, Winfrey was discovered to be very intelligent and was given grant money to attend college. Excelling in the communications program at Tennessee State University, she worked at a local TV station delivering the news. She went on to be the youngest news anchor and the first black female news anchor in Nashville. She also worked as a co-host for a local talk show and a game show . Her AM Chicago talk show flew to the top of the charts over the longer-running *Donahue Show* and it was only a matter of time before she hosted her own show and the mega entertainment industry that includes magazines, books, websites, radio and film. A true rags-to-riches story for sure.

Quote: Whatever you fear most, has no power—it is your fear that has the power.

36. Dr. David Michael Burns—Graduating from Harvard Medical School in 1972, he has devoted his life to treating lung diseases caused by cigarette smoking and also caring for those who suffer. He actually testified in the U.S. Department of Justice Civil Case against all major tobacco companies in February of 2001. He is a faculty Professor and Medical Director of Respiratory Therapy at the University of California San Diego. From 1980 to 1983, Burns was Scientific Editor of the *Surgeon's General's Report* and from 1984 to 1987 he was Senior Scientific Editor of the same, as well as a contributor to all the *Surgeon General's Reports* on smoking since 1975. He started and has been the head of the Tobacco Control Policies Project. Like I said, his life is all about smokers and how to help them medically, legislatively and personally. Surgeon General C. Everett Koop awarded him the Surgeon General's Medallion for "actions of exceptional achievement in the cause of public health and medicine." He has served on the World Health Organizations Scientific Advisory Committee on Tobacco, has been a consultant with the Department of Health and Human Services for 27 years, and a consultant with the National Cancer Institute. Thank you, Dr. Burns for contributing unstintingly.

Quote: Remember that fear always lurks behind perfectionism. Confronting your fears and allowing yourself the right to be human, can, paradoxically, make you a far happier and more productive person.

35. Nora Dorothy Bernard (1890-1955)--Born in Port Elizabeth, South Africa, she was a silent movie actress from 1910 to 1913, appearing in sixteen films. Her father, William Bernard, was born in Auckland, New Zealand and was a stock company manager as well as a popular actor in his own right. Her mother, Roy Elizabeth Ayrd was born in Sligo, Ireland. I wonder how those two ever met? Dorothy or "Dot" grew up in Portland, Oregon as an only child and performed in several plays at the Baker Theater Company. When she was fifteen, her family moved to Los Angeles, California and her father worked at the Balasco Theater. In 1909, she married another actor, A.H. Van Buren and they had one daughter, Marjorie "Midge" Van Buren.

Quote: Courage is fear that has said its prayers.

34. Taylor Alison Swift (1989)—Born in Reading, Pennsylvania, Miss Swift was raised on a Christmas tree farm and had a maternal grandmother who was an opera singer. At the age of 10, a computer repairman showed her the fingerings for three chords on her guitar and she wrote her first song, "Lucky You" at the age of 12. The family moved to Nashville when she turned 14 and she was homeschooled for part of her high school years. Previously she had tried to sign with the Nashville studios when she was only 11, but no one was interested. Finally at 15, she was hired by Sony/ATV Tree Publishing House and became the youngest songwriter they had ever had on staff. In 2006, her first recorded song, "Tim McGraw" debuted on the Billboard 200 and she was on her way. Clearly this girl was born with a gift.

Quote: "Fearless" is living in spite of those things that scare you to death.

33. Marie Sklodowska Curie (1867-1934)—Born in Poland, Miss Curie was a woman of firsts: first woman to win a Nobel Prize, only woman to win in two fields (physics and chemistry), only person to win in multiple sciences, first female professor at the University of Paris, first woman to discover a chemical element (Polonium—named after her native country), and first and only woman to be interred in the Pantheon in Paris (alongside such dignitaries as Louis Braille, Victor Hugo and Voltaire). She also discovered another element that she and her husband named Radium—"for its intense radio activity." Sadly, her research on radioactivity lead to her untimely death at age 66 from aplastic anemia, caused by the very compounds she was working with. At that time, no one realized the effects of Radium. Her research papers are too dangerous to work with and even her cookbook is too contaminated to touch. Those who wish to consult them must wear protective clothing.

Quote: Nothing in life is to be feared, it is only to be understood.

32. Rosa Louise McCauley Parks (1913-2005)—Born in Tuskegee, Alabama, Miss Parks was of African-American, Cherokee-Creek and Scots-Irish descent. U. S. Congress called her "The First Lady of Civil Rights" and "The Mother of the Freedom Movement." Her claim-to-fame came in December of 1955 when she refused to give her seat on a bus to a white person in Montgomery, Alabama. She was arrested and sent to jail. After her release, she joined with Martin Luther King, Jr. to bring the Civil Rights Movement into the national spotlight. One year after her arrest, she had the privilege of riding another bus in Montgomery on the day public transportation was legally integrated. She lived to be 92 years old and some of the many honors she received during her lifetime were the Presidential Medal of Freedom, the Congressional Gold Medal and a place in the National Statuary Hall in the Capitol Building in Washington, D.C. alongside Henry Clay, Helen Keller, Sam Houston and Sequoyah.

Quote: I have learned over the years that when one's mind is made up, this diminishes fear; knowing what must be done does away with fear.

31. George Walton Lucas, Jr. (1944)—Born in Modesto, California, Lucas is best-known as the creator of two mega movie series—*Star Wars* and *Indiana Jones*. His first film was *American Graffiti*, which inspired the popular TV series *Happy Days* as well as introducing us to future *Indiana Jones* star, Harrison Ford. His early career plans centered on race car driving, but a near-fatal accident just before high school graduation cured him of that. He went to college to study anthropology, but got hooked on cinematography while taking a liberal arts class. After transferring to the University of Southern California School of Cinematic Arts, he met Steven Spielberg and the rest, as they say, is history. He has won many awards including the American Film Institute Life Achievement Award and Discovery Channel's 100 Greatest Americans Award, as well as being inducted into the Science Fiction Hall of Fame and the California Hall of Fame. *Star Wars* is the third-highest-grossing film series of all time, following *Harry Potter* and *James Bond*.

Quote: Train yourself to let go of the things you fear to lose.

30. King Solomon (970-931 BC)—Born in Hebron, 30 miles south of Jerusalem, he was the favored son of King David and, in fact, became king after him. Many consider him the wisest man who ever lived, a gift given to him when God said, *"Ask for whatever you want."* (1Kings 3:5) Throughout his long reign, he solved many dilemmas, including the one between two women who claimed the same infant. Solomon simply said, *"Cut the living child in two and give each one half."* When one of the women protested, saying, *"Please give her the living baby! Don't kill him!"* he knew her to be the rightful mother (1 Kings 3:16-28). He built the first Temple in Jerusalem in 957 BC to replace the tent sanctuary that Moses had used in the Sinai Desert (1 Kings 6). Solomon also wrote three books in the Bible--

Proverbs: a book of wisdom covering the subjects of relationships, money, sex and business; Ecclesiastes: a book that instructs us to look to God and not to things; and the Song of Solomon: a love poem. He had an amazing 700 wives and 300 concubines and their foreign religions ultimately led him away from God and his kingdom was torn in two.

Quote: Now all has been heard; here is the conclusion of the matter: Fear God and keep His commandments, for this is the whole duty of man. **Ecclesiastes 12:13 (NIV)**

29. Publilius Syrus (1st Century BC)—Born in Syria, Syrus was taken as a slave to Italy. When his new master discovered how intelligent he was, he freed him and had him educated. He actually won a prize from the hand of Caesar for his part in an improvisation put on to entertain the ruling class. He wrote maxims, or wise sayings, the most famous of which is "The judge is condemned when the guilty is acquitted." Another, more familiar, is "A rolling stone gathers no moss." 700 of his maxims were published in a book entitled, *The Sentences*, which is still in print today. He reminds me of Aesop, who was also a slave, and wrote clever fables.

Quote: The fear of death is more to be dreaded than death itself.

28. Leslie "Les" Brown (1945)—Born on the floor of an abandoned building in the poorest section of Miami, Florida, Les and his twin brother, Wes, were adopted by Mamie Brown. She was a cafeteria worker and struggled to make ends meet. He says of her, "All that I am and all that I ever hoped to be, I owe to my mother." He was declared "educably mentally retarded" due to lack of attention in school and uncontrollable energy (today we would call that ADHD). This crushed his self-esteem for many years, but with the support of his mother, he finished high school. Starting out on his own, he slept on the floor of a rented office in Chicago. Eventually, he built his own public-speaking enterprise and went on to record a series of speeches for the Public Broadcasting System as well as emceeing local banquets. He served in the Ohio Legislature for three terms and today speaks to Fortune 500 Companies and audiences numbering up to 80,000. From these humble beginnings, he now travels the world and brings inspiration to millions.

Quote: Fear does not have any special power unless you empower it by submitting to it.

27. King David (1040 BC)—Born in Bethlehem, he first came to prominence when he battled the giant Goliath, who had been mocking God and the Israelite army in *1 Samuel 17*. He started out as a shepherd for his father, Jesse, and killed lions and bears to protect the flock. He was very skilled with the Old Testament weapon of a sling and stones—that's how he killed the giant, with God's help, of course. Israel's present king, Saul, takes notice and makes David one of his elite fighting men. David goes on to defeat many foes and after Saul's suicide, becomes the new king. He builds a fabulous kingdom in Jerusalem and returns the Ark of the Covenant to the people in *2 Samuel 6.* But he has many wives, and children that fight each other and him. In fact, he had to command his army to stop the revolt of one son, Absolom, who died trying to escape from David's general, Abner. His life was filled with overwhelming grief, as well as much happiness, but his greatest disappointment was that he did not build the Temple of the Lord (his son, Solomon, got that honor). David wrote the Book of Psalms in the Bible and his poems go from highest joy to lowest despair. God said of him, *"I have found David son of Jesse a man after my own heart."* (Acts 13:2 KJV)

Quote: In God, whose word I praise, in God I trust; I will not fear. What can mortal man do to me?
Psalms 56:4 (NIV)

26. Albert Einstein (1879-1955)--Born in Ulm, Germany, Einstein is known as the greatest physicist who ever lived. In fact, his name is synonymous with "genius." His father was an engineer and manufactured electrical equipment. As a young child he built models and mechanical devices for fun. In school in Switzerland, he tested perfect in both physics and math. He met his first wife, Mileva Maric at college in Zurich. She was the only woman enrolled in the Physics and Mathematics program there. Married in 1903, they had one daughter, Lieserl and two sons, Hans Albert (who went on to be a famous engineer in his own right) and Eduard. After graduation he took a job reviewing patents for electromagnetic devices. His second wife was also his first cousin, Elsa (Einstein) Lowenthal. It was after he wrote papers on relativity of matter and energy that he became known in Europe. Then he taught at various colleges until he proposed the theory that the sun's gravity could bend light from distant stars. This paper made him famous around the world and he traveled and lectured for several years before making America his permanent home. Coming from a Jewish family, he gave up his German citizenship after Hitler came into power, and became an American citizen in 1940. He loved the musical genius of Mozart and played the violin with great feeling. After the war, he was asked to be President of Israel, but declined. He won the Nobel Prize in Physics in 1921, "Person of the Century" in *Time Magazine* and had element #99 named after him, "Einsteinium." He died in 1995 of a heart aneurysm and his brain has been preserved for scientific study.

Quote: There are only two ways to live your life. One is as though nothing is a miracle.
The other is as though everything is a miracle.

(this is my favorite quote)

25. Publilius Syrus—Please see #29.

Quote: Tis foolish to fear what you cannot avoid.

24. Ellen Goodman (1941)--Born in Newton, Massachusetts, she was a Pulitzer Prize-winning magazine columnist and American journalist. She graduated cum laude (highest honors) from Radcliffe College, a part of Harvard College, with a Degree in Modern European History. She worked for *Newsweek, Detroit Free Press* and was associate editor of the *Boston Globe*. She had one daughter, Katie, with her first husband, Anthony Goodman. Katie is a musical comedian. Her second husband was journalist Bob Levey. Ms. Goodman published eight books and retired in 2010.

Quote: The central struggle of parenthood is to let our hopes for our children outweigh our fears.

23. Eric Hoffer (1902-1983)--Born in Bronx, New York, his parents emmigrated from Alsace, France. His father was a cabinetmaker. When he was 5, his mother fell down the stairs with him in her arms and he was blind until the age of 15. Receiving the gift of sight for the second time, he determined to read all he could in case he lost it again. His mother died as the result of that fall and when his father died shortly after he was 15, he used the insurance money to go to Los Angeles. He lived on skid row and worked odd jobs. He also spent time as a migrant worker, went prospecting for gold and worked as a longshoreman. He tried to join the armed forces but was rejected because of a hernia. During his travels, he collected library cards from each town that he visited, wrote two semi-autobiographical novels and a long article about his experiences in a federal work camp. Coming from a working class background, Hoffer felt that people on welfare as well as the very rich should have to spend two years of their life in a national service program to gain maturity. He wrote eleven books and received the Presidential Medal of Freedom from Ronald Reagan. There is also an Eric Hoffer Award for books and prose. He died in 1983 at the age of 80 years.

Quote: You can discover what your enemy fears most by observing the means he uses to frighten you.

22. Aung San Suu Kyi (1945)--Born in Rangoon (now called Yangon), Burma, she is the daughter of Aung San, who founded the modern Burmese Army and worked to achieve independence from the British Empire in 1947. He was assassinated that same year. Suu Kyi grew up with her mother; Burmese

Ambassador to India and Nepal, and one brother. Sadly, her other brother drowned in a lake at the age of eight. Her surviving brother emmigrated to San Diego, California. She attended college in New Delhi and Oxford and earned degrees in Philosophy, Politics and Economics. She worked at the UN in New York City and married Dr. Michael Aris, a scholar of Tibetan culture in 1972. They had two sons while Suu Kyi earned her PhD at the University of London. In 1988 she returned to Burma to care for her elderly mother and her husband was denied entry visas by the new dictatorship. They never saw each other again. Her children, living in the United Kingdom were allowed to visit only rarely. She founded the National League for Democracy in 1988 and spent 15 out of 21 years under house arrest. While traveling with party members she was attacked two times, threatened with assassination and put in prison. Finally in April of 2012, Suu Kyi won a seat in Parliament and lobbies today to overturn restrictive laws, reinstate democratic rights and elect an independent judiciary. She won the Nobel Peace Prize in 1991 for her "non-violent struggle for democracy and human rights."

Quote: The only real prison is fear, and the only real freedom is freedom from fear.

21. Angela Louise Wozniak (1948-2008)--Born in Minneapolis, her father was the well-known "Grandpa Judge," Daniel Donald Wozniak. He first served as a State Representative from 1950 to 1965 and then was appointed Ambassador Select to Ecuador. He joined the Bench in 1982. Ms. Wozniak attended Georgetown Visitation Preparatory School in Washington D.C. and Hamline University in St. Paul, Minnesota. She was very involved in political activism and was a lobbyist instrumental in getting the law "Safe Place for Newborns Program" passed. In Minnesota this law states that a parent can safely surrender their unharmed newborn up to 3 days old at any hospital without fear of prosecution. The baby is then given medical treatment, if needed, and turned over to County Social Services for foster care and/or adoption. She had three children of her own; Angela, Douglas and Faith.

Quote: I have come to realize that my trouble with living has come from fear and smallness within me.

20. Edmund Burke (1729-1797)--Born in Dublin, Ireland, his father was solicitor of the Church of Ireland and he was raised as a Protestant. His sister, Juliana was raised as a Catholic, like their mother, Mary Nagle. Years later, Parliament members tried to disqualify him from service by accusing him of being a Catholic. His early education was formed in a Quaker school in nearby Ballitore and he attended Trinity College in Dublin. While there, he organized a Debating Club which soon joined with the Historical Club to become the College Historical Society, the oldest undergraduate society in the world. Burke's meeting minutes are still on display at the college. He graduated in 1748 and his father wanted him to be a lawyer, but instead he took up historical writing, his first published book being; *A Vindication of*

Natural Society: A View of the Miseries and Evils Arising to Mankind. (1756). He became a member of the British Parliament in 1765, while continuing to write. He was especially interested in the controversy with the American Colonies and showed his support for their grievances in his 1774 speech, which included the comment: "Be content to bind America by laws of trade—but do not burthen them with taxes." Again in 1775 he stated; "The people of the Colonies are descendants of Englishmen. They are devoted to liberty according to English ideas and principles." During this time, he predicted some "extraordinary convulsion" in France. He was known as the Father of Modern Anglo-Conservatism, supported Irish Catholics and Indians and had a statue in his memory erected in Washington, D.C. Winston Churchill called him an "Apostle of Liberty."

Quote: *No passion so effectually robs the mind of all its powers of acting and reasoning as fear.*

19. George Sewell (1924-2007)--Born in Hoxton, part of London's East End, his father was a printer and his mother a florist. He left school at age 14 and apprenticed with his father. Work was slow, so he soon began repairing houses damaged by the bombings of WWII. He joined the Royal Air Force and became a pilot, but too late to serve in the war. Then it was the Merchant Navy for him as a steward on the HMS Queen Mary and also the HMS Queen Elizabeth as they crossed back and forth over the Atlantic Ocean. He spent some time as a street photographer, an assistant to a French roller-skating team, a drummer and assistant road manager for a rumba band and finally traveled all over England as a courier for a motor coach company (reminds me of Jack London). It wasn't until a chance meeting with a famous actor at age 35 that his career in the theater began. From his first small role in *Fings Ain't Wot They Used to Be,* his career prospered until a play he was in traveled to Paris and even Broadway. For many years he starred in various television series about crime and law enforcement. Sewell married Helen and they had one daughter, Elizabeth.

Quote: *Fear is that tax that conscience pays to guilt.*

18. Henry Wadsworth Longfellow (1807-1882)--Born in Portland, Maine, he was the son of Stephen, a lawyer. His mother, Zilpah Wadsworth, had a father who was a general in the American Revolution and a member of Congress. At the tender age of 3, he began attending a local "dame school," a sort of elementary school before public schools came into being. At age 6, he entered Portland Academy and excelled in Latin. The Portland *Gazette* printed his first poem at age 13. Longfellow entered Bowdoin College when he was 15 and it was there that he met Nathaniel Hawthorne, who became a friend for life. During his senior year, he wrote in a letter to his father; "I most eagerly aspire after future eminence in literature." While at Bowdoin, he had over 40 poems and essays published in various newspapers and magazines. He ranked fourth in his class and gave the commencement address. After graduation, the college offered him a professorship if he would complete a tour in Europe first. He was gone for three years and in his travels became fluent in French, Spanish, Portuguese and German. It was during this time that he also met Washington Irving. While teaching at Bowdoin, he married Mary Potter, bur sadly she died after a miscarriage four years later. He memorialized their love in the poem, *Footsteps of Angels*. In 1934, Harvard offered him the job of Professor of Modern Languages, but once again asked him to tour Europe before assuming his duties. This time he learned the Dutch, Danish, Swedish, Finnish and Icelandic languages. After taking over his new job, he married again, this time to Frances Appleton, and they had six children. Sadly, her dress caught on fire and she died of her burns. At the time, Longfellow sustained burns on his face trying to get the fire out and began to wear a long beard. He wrote the poem, *Evening Star* for her and *Cross of Snow* eighteen years later while still mourning. Some of his famous poems were *Paul Revere's Ride, The Courtship of Miles Standish* (I'm actually related to him), and *The Song of Hiawatha*. He wrote over sixteen poetry collections, plays, travelogues, translations and anthologies. Longfellow was the first non-British writer to be commemorated with a bust in the Poet's Corner at Westminster Abbey.

Quote: Look not mournfully into the past. It comes not back again. Wisely improve the present. It is thine. Go forth to meet the shadowy future, without fear.

17. George Herman "Babe" Ruth, Jr. (1895-1948)--Born in Pigtown, a poor suburb of Baltimore, Maryland, George Herman Ruth, Jr. was the son of German-American parents George, Sr. and Kate Schamberger. They owned saloons and sold lightning rods. His mother died young of tuberculosis and only one of his seven siblings survived past infancy. At the age of 7, his father signed him over to the St. Mary's Industrial School for Boys, a type of orphanage/reformatory school. Brother Matthias Boutlier, Head of Discipline at the school, took him under his wing and introduced him to baseball. While at the school, Ruth was taught the trade of tailoring and was involved in band and drama. But at baseball he always excelled. In fact, during one game against St. Mary's University, former student, Joe Engel, was in the stands. Impressed with Ruth's pitching skills, he brought him to the attention of Baltimore Orioles owner, Jack Dunn. He was drafted at $250 per month, which would equal about $5,900 today, on Valentine's Day, 1914. Since he was only 19, the other players called him "Jack Dunn's baby" and his nickname was born. Within the year he was sold to the Boston Red Sox and then he went to the New York Yankees. And you know the rest of the story. During this time, he played beside the famous Lou Gehrig and helped the Yankees win seven pennants and four World Series titles. Ranked as the third-greatest U.S. Athlete of the Century behind Michael Jordan and Muhammad Ali, Ruth hit 714 home runs and was one of the first five players to be inducted into the National Baseball Hall of Fame. Babe Ruth and his first wife, Helen Woodruff, adopted one daughter, Dorothy. His second wife, actress Claire Merritt had a daughter, Julia from her first marriage, and he adopted her as well.

Quote: Never let the fear of striking out get in your way.

16. James Douglas "Jim" Morrison (1943-1971)--Born in Melbourne, Florida, he was the son of Rear Admiral George Stephen Morrison. As a consequence of his father being in the Navy, the family moved a lot. He attended many different schools in many different states including Alameda High School in California, and he ultimately graduated from George Washington High School in Alexandria, Virginia. He went to college at St. Petersburg University and Florida State University, where he was arrested for playing a drunken prank. He received an undergraduate degree in Theater Arts from University of California, Los Angeles (UCLA) and made several short films. But he loved to write poetry and later many of these were used for songs when he joined the blues/rock group *The Doors*. Struggling with a severe alcohol addiction, Morrison died at age 27. He published four books of poetry.

Quote: Expose yourself to your deepest fear; after that, fear has no power, and the fear of freedom shrinks and vanishes. You are free.

15. Franklin Delano Roosevelt (1882-1945)—Born into the wealthy Roosevelt family, Hyde Park, New York was the birthplace of our 32nd president. His parents, James and Sara Delano were sixth cousins and his father was 54 when he was born. The family made many trips to Europe and young Franklin spoke German and French fluently. He also learned to shoot, ride horses, row, sail and play polo, lawn tennis and golf. He attended Groton school in Massachusetts, along with other students from wealthy families. The headmaster there spoke daily about helping the less fortunate and this led to Roosevelt's plan for the New Deal when he became president. In Harvard College he maintained a C average and was Editor-in-Chief of the college newspaper. While in college, his 5th cousin, Theodore became President of the United States. He met his 5th cousin-once-removed, Eleanor, at a White House reception and they were engaged at the ages of 21 and 19. They married while he was in Columbia Law School and had six children while he worked at a Wall Street Firm. Before his presidency, he was in the State Senate, served as Assistant Secretary of the Navy and ran for Vice-President with James Cox. They lost the 1920 Presidential Election to Warren G. Harding. While vacationing with his family in Canada in 1921, he contracted polio. He bought the resort at Warm Springs, Georgia to undergo hydrotherapy and this facility still treats about 5,000 patients per year. He also founded the National Foundation for Infantile Paralysis, or March of Dimes, to fund these treatments. Then he was Governor of New York for three years before being elected president during the Great Depression. When he took office, ¼ of the workforce was unemployed, 2 million people were homeless, and 48 states had closed their banks.

His "New Deal" Civilian Conservation Corps (CCC) put 250,000 unemployed people to work on rural local projects. The WPA, or Works Progress Administration gave relief (or welfare) to millions while they waited to find jobs. Social Security was started and Prohibition was repealed. During his fourth term, the Japanese bombed Pearl Harbor and America entered the war. Sixteen warships were damaged or destroyed and 3,000 people lost their lives. In America, first generation Germans, Japanese and Italians were interred in camps for fear of their involvement with the Axis powers. Roosevelt died at Warm Springs before he finished his last term in 1945. The Franklin Delano Roosevelt Memorial in

Washington, DC states: *Freedom of Speech, Freedom of Worship, Freedom From Want and Freedom From Fear.*

Quote: The only thing we have to fear is fear itself.

14. Ann E. Bray (1994-2010)

Quote: Never fear spoiling children by making them too happy. Happiness is the atmosphere in which all good affections glow.

13. William Shakespeare (1564-1616)--Born in Stratford-Upon-Avon (Street Over Avon River), England, his father was an alderman and made gloves. His mother, Mary Arden, was the daughter of a wealthy farmer and had eight children, of which William was the eldest son. He attended King's New School (an early English Grammar School) where he learned Latin grammar and studied Latin Classical authors. Not much else is known about him until a marriage license was issued to Anne Hathaway (26) and William Shakespeare (18) on November 27, 1582. They had three children: a daughter, Susanna, who married Dr. John Hall; Hamnet, who died at age 11 and Judith, his twin, who married Thomas Quiney, a vintner. In the late 1500's, Shakespeare's career as an actor, playwright and poet really took off in London, 102 miles away from his home. He became part-owner of the playing company known as Lord Chamberlain's Men, later changed to The King's Men, that played in the Globe Theatre. There many of his 16 comedies, 10 histories and 12 tragedies were enacted and enjoyed by street urchins as well as the highest society in the land. When all of the theaters in London closed during the Black Plague, Shakespeare had the time to write several narrative poems, the most well-known being his 154 *Sonnets*, which were first published in 1609. A "folio" of his 38 plays was published in 1623; the most famous of them being *Romeo and Juliet, Hamlet* and *The Tempest.* He died at age 52 and was buried in the same church that he was baptized in as an infant; Holy Trinity Church in Stratford, sometimes referred to as Shakespeare's Church. A monument erected there in 1623 compared him to Nestor, Socrates and Virgil. In his will, he left the bulk of his estate to his eldest daughter, Susanna, with the provision that she leave the money to "the first son of her body." She had no surviving children, nor did her sister, Judith. So, Shakespeare's direct line was ended at his death. He is known today as England's National Poet and The Bard of Avon.

Quote: Present fears are less than horrible imaginings.

12. Author Unknown or Anonymous—We do not know who said or penned these lines.

Quote: We promise according to our hopes and perform according to our fears.

11. John Henry Cardinal Newman (1801-1890)--Born in London, he was the son of John Newman, a banker and Jemima Fourdrinier, whose family were Huguenot refugees from France. He was the eldest of three sons and three daughters. At the age of 7 he entered the Great Ealing School where he was taught mathematics and read the classics. He did not participate in any sports and spent his free time reading Walter Scott and Robert Southey. When he was 15, he had a conversion experience that he called "more certain than that I have hands and feet." He began studying the writings of John Calvin and Luther's proclamation of "justification by faith alone," and this became his creed. He spent four years at Trinity College at Oxford and graduated third in his class. He became a Deacon at Christ Church Cathedral at Oxford and was ordained a priest there. Taking over the Curate of St. Clement's Church, he began to write on evangelical matters. In 1832 he traveled throughout Europe and began to write poetry, some of which was used in later hymns. When his writings were contested in 1842, he resigned all of his religious posts and retreated to a house in Littlemore—soon to be called Newman College. Two years later he converted to Roman Catholicism and lived a secluded life in Ireland, teaching at the University College in Dublin. He died of pneumonia in 1890 and chose these words for his gravestone: *Heart Speaks to Heart.* He left for posterity over 40 books, letter and tracts.

Quote: Fear not that life shall come to an end, but rather fear that it shall never have a beginning.

10. John Alfred Spender (1862-1942)--Born in Bath, England, he was the eldest of four sons. His father was a doctor and his mother was the famous English novelist, Lillian Spender, who wrote 18 books. Spender attended Bath College and then Balliol College in Oxford. He instructors wanted him to be a lawyer, but he wanted to be a journalist. His first writing job was as Senior Editor for *The Echo*, followed by the Editorship of a daily newspaper, *The Eastern Morning News.* When this was sold, he took some time out to write his first book, *The State and Pensions of Old Age.* Then he became the Editor of the *Pall Mall Gazette* and worked there until it was sold to William Waldorf Astor (my great-grandmother was a tutor to his children). He married and was hired as Editor for the prominent newspaper, *The Westminster Gazette.* Spender was instrumental in getting it acknowledged as "the best edited paper in London." He retired at age 60 and devoted the rest of his life to writing histories, travelogues, biographies and memoirs. He and his wife had no children. He was awarded the Companion of Honor by the ruling monarch of Great Britain which is given for "nationally important service and outstanding achievement in the arts, literature, music, science, politics, industry or religion." Their motto is: *In Action Faithful, and in Honor Clear.*

Quote: Fear God, yes, but don't be afraid of Him.

9. Anna Eleanor Roosevelt Roosevelt (1884-1962)--Born in New York City to Elliot Roosevelt, son of Teddy Roosevelt and Anna Hall, Eleanor had two brothers, Elliot, Jr. and Hall. The Roosevelt families were very wealthy, but all the money couldn't save her mother and brother when they died of diphtheria in 1902. Her father passed away two years later due to alcoholism. She was raised by her mother's mother, Mary Ludlow Hall and had a very lonely childhood. At 14, she felt that she was ugly and wrote, "No matter how plain a woman may be, if truth and loyalty are stamped upon her face, all will be attracted to her." She was sent to a private finishing school in London and learned to speak French. When she returned, her family gave her a fancy debutante ball at the Waldorf-Astoria Hotel and then she turned her back on riches and volunteered as a social worker in the slums of New York. At 17 she met her distant cousin, Franklin Delano Roosevelt and two years later they were engaged and then married on St. Patrick's Day in 1905. For their honeymoon, they traveled in Europe for three months. Eleanor had six children: Anna, James, FDR, Jr. who died at 7 months, Elliott, FDR, Jr. again, and then John. After her husband contracted polio, she was by his side through everything political until he was elected President of the United States. After his death, she continued with her activism for civil rights, was a co-founder of Freedom House and Delegate to the UN General Assembly from 1945 to 1952; having been appointed by President Harry Truman. Eleanor was an international author and speaker and has been called First Lady of the World. On Gallup's Most Widely Admired People of the 20th Century," she ranked #10 after Mother Teresa, Martin Luther King, Jr., John F. Kennedy, Albert Einstein, Helen Keller, Franklin Delano Roosevelt, Billy Graham and Pope John Paul II.

Quote: You gain strength, courage and confidence by every experience in which you really stop to look fear in the face. You are able to say to yourself, "I have lived through this horror; I can take the next thing that comes along." You must do the thing you think you cannot do.

8. Elbert Hubbard (1856-1915)--Born in Bloomington, Illinois, he was the son of Dr. Silas and Juliana Frances (Frank) Hubbard. His older brother, Charlie, fell when he was young and died at only 9 years of age. His older sister, Hannah Frances was nicknamed "Frank" like his mother and he had three younger sisters; Mary, Anna and Honor. Attendance at a local public school showed him excelling in spelling, fractions and checkers--his sisters said he was a troublemaker. His first job was as a traveling salesman selling Larkin Soap and he came up with the idea of paying premiums and leaving samples behind for trial use. With his first wife, Bertha Crawford, he founded Roycroft, an arts and crafts community in East Aurora, New York. The town consisted of the Roycroft Press, which published two magazines, printed books on homemade paper and also ran a bindery to make books for other people. Most of Hubbard's seven books were printed there. Other businesses included a furniture shop specializing in the Mission-style, a Leather Shop, a shop offering hand-hammered copper goods and a traveling carpenter. There is a museum there now that commemorates their accomplishments and has furniture and decorative items from that era on display in the George and Gladys Scheidemantle House, which was listed on the National Register of Historic Places in 1993. In his books and in his life, Hubbard was a great supporter of free-enterprise and good old American know-how. When the *Titanic* sunk in 1912, he wrote a stirring account of the bravery of those who were lost and those who survived. Ironically, three years later he and his second wife, Alice Moore, lost their lives when the *Lusitania* was sunk by German torpedoes. His son, Elbert Hubbard, Jr., continued to run the Roycroft shops for 23 more years. A 360-page book was published at Roycroft Press to commemorate his life and was titled; *In Memoriam: Elbert and Alice Hubbard*. It included testimonials from then-famous and well-known individuals such as; J. Ogden Armour (hot dogs), Luther Burbank (botanist), W. Atlee Burpee (garden seeds), Henry J. Heinz (ketchup), James Whitcomb Riley (poet), Billy Sunday (evangelist) and Booker T. Washington (black leader).

Quote: The greatest mistake you can make in life is to be continually fearing you will make one.

7. Real Live Preacher--Gordon Atkinson was a Baptist preacher for many years in San Antonio, Texas before starting the anonymous blog, Real Live Preacher in 2002. He resigned his pastorate to devote more time to writing with the dual goals of writing honestly and well. His most popular blogs are *The Preacher's Story* and *The Raccoon Stories* and you can read these on his website. Atkinson has written three books, *Real Live Preacher.com*, *Turtles All the Way Down* and *The Christmas Story You've Never Heard*. He also designs and manages Drupal Websites for a company in Australia.

Quote: One of the joys we have in being human is in exercising our freedom to choose and to take each case as it comes to us. We are not robots who are forced into behaviors by their programming. We see things; we think about things; and we choose our course of action or beliefs appropriately. And as long as that remains true of us, we will live every day of our lives on one slippery slope or another. There is no reason to fear this.

6. King Solomon—Please see #30.

Quote: The fear of the Lord is the beginning of wisdom, and knowledge of the Holy One is understanding. Proverbs 9:10 (NIV)

5. Amy Tan (1952)—Born in Oakland, California, she is the daughter of Chinese immigrants; Daisy Li and John Tan, a Baptist minister. Her mother was formerly married to an abusive man in China and left three daughters behind when she fled for her life. Her most popular book, *The Joy Luck* Club is based on this story. When Amy was 15, both her father and older brother, Peter, died of brain tumors. She moved with her mother and younger brother, John, Jr. to Switzerland, where she finished her high school education. In 1987, she and her mother returned to China and she met her three half-sisters for the very first time. At San Jose State University she received her B.A. and M.A. in English and completed Doctoral Linguistics Studies at the University College of Santa Cruz and University College of Berkley. She is married to a tax accountant that she met on a blind date, Louis DeMattei. She has won many book awards including finalist in the National Book Award, National Book Critics Circle Award and the *Los Angeles Times* Fiction Prize. Also the American Library Association Notable Books and Best Book for Young Adults.

Quote: You see what power is—holding someone else's fear in your hand and showing it to them.

4. William Shakespeare—Please see # 13.

Quote: Present fears are less than horrible imaginings.

3. Timothy (17-97 AD)—Born in Lystra, Turkey of a Greek father and a Jewish mother, Timothy was a companion to the apostle Paul on his many missionary journeys and was in charge of transcribing letters for him. Paul reminded him in his first epistle, *"Don't let anyone look down on you because you are young, but set an example for the believers in speech, in life, in love, in faith and in purity."* 1 Timothy 4:12 and also reminded him of his godly heritage in 2 Timothy 1:5—*"I have been reminded of your sincere faith, which first lived in your grandmother Lois and in your mother Eunice and, I am persuaded, now lives in you also."* Timothy was noted for his vast knowledge of the Scriptures and was jailed for his faith at least once. Paul selected Timothy as Bishop of Ephesus and his official Feast Day is January 22. He was killed at 80 years of age while attempting to stop a pagan parade. They dragged him through the streets and stoned him to death.

Quote: For God did not give us a spirit of timidity, but a spirit of power, of love and of self-discipline.
2 Timothy 1:7 (NIV)

2. Ralph Waldo Emerson (1803-1882)—Born in Boston, Massachusetts, his mother was Ruth Haskins and his father was the Reverend William Emerson, a Unitarian minister. He had four brothers; William, Edward, Robert and Charles—Edward and Charles succumbed to tuberculosis before they were grown and Phebe, John and Mary died in early childhood. When Emerson was 8, his father died of stomach cancer and he was raised by his mother and much-beloved Aunt Mary Moody Emerson. He attended Boston Latin School and then Harvard College at the age of 14. He always kept a list of the books he read (I do that!) and started a journal which eventually was compiled in *Wide World*. As the Class Poet, he was required to read an original poem on Harvard's Class Day. He then attended Harvard Divinity School after which he married Ellen Louisa Tucker. She died two years later. Emerson was devastated and left his ministerial career behind to become a lecturer and teacher. He toured Europe and wrote about his travels in *English Trails*. Returning to America, he married again (Lydia Jackson) and they had four children; Waldo, Ellen, Edith and Edward. Sadly, Waldo died of scarlet fever. He bought 11 acres near the fabled Walden Pond of his best friend, Henry David Thoreau, and hit the newly-created lecture tour. He gave about 80 lectures per year at a cost of $10 to $15 each and delivered around 1500 in his lifetime. Over the course of ten years he slowly began losing his memory (dementia or Alzheimer's?) and died of pneumonia at the age of 79. He is buried in the Sleepy Hollow Cemetery in Concord, Massachusetts. Known as the *Concord Sage*, he published 10 Collections, 10 Essays and 2 Poems; *Concord Hymn* being the most famous.

Quote: He has not learned the lesson of life who does not every day surmount a fear.

And finally--#1!

Job—*"In the land of Uz there lived a man whose name was Job. This man was blameless and upright; he feared God and shunned evil"* Job 1:1. He had seven sons and three daughters and everything was perfect in his life. God mentioned this one day and Satan accused Him of protecting Job and said that if things started to go wrong, he would desert God. So God told Satan to do what he wanted with Job as long as he spared his life. Thus began a long struggle against fate as Job lost his children, his riches, his friends and his health. His wife even told him to curse God and die. But Job persevered and was rewarded in the end with more children, more riches and more blessings than he had ever had before. There are 42 chapters chronicling the struggles of Job and it helps to read these when you think you are having a hard time, especially when suffering grief. After his trial he lived 140 more years and saw his descendants down to the fourth generation.

Quote: Then Job replied: "Their homes are safe and free from fear; the rod of the Lord is not upon them." Job 21:9 (NIV).

Complete List of all the "Fear nots" (NIV)

Here are all 80 verses in the Bible that have the words **"Fear not"** in them. So, I guess you can count back 80 days before your scary event and read one each day. Why not get out a spiral notebook and write down how *you* felt during the process? Then you would write a book too!

Genesis 15:1—*After this, the word of the Lord came to Abram in a vision: "**Do not be afraid**, Abram, I am your shield, your very great reward."*

Genesis 21:17—*God heard the boy crying, and the angel of God called to Hagar from heaven and said to her, "What is the matter, Hagar? **Do not be afraid**; God has heard the boy crying as he lies there. Lift the boy up and take him by the hand, for I will make him into a great nation."*

Genesis 26:24—*That night the Lord appeared to Isaac and said, "I am the God of your father Abraham. **Do not be afraid**, for I am with you; I will bless you and will increase the number of your descendants for the sake of my servant Abraham."*

Genesis 35:17-18—*And as Rachel was having great difficulty in childbirth, the midwife said to her, "**Don't be afraid**, for you have another son." As she breathed her last—for she was dying—she named her son Ben-Oni (son of my trouble). But his father named him Benjamin.*

Genesis 43:23—*"It's alright," Joseph said (to his brothers). "**Do not be afraid**. Your God, the God of your father, has given you treasure in your sacks; I received your silver." Then he brought Simeon out to them.*

Genesis 46:3—*"I am the God, the God of your father," he said (to Jacob). "**Do not be afraid** to go down to Egypt, for I will make you into a great nation there. I will go down to Egypt with you, and I will surely bring you back again. And Joseph's own hand will close your eyes.*

Genesis 50:19-21—*But Joseph said to them, "**Do not be afraid**. Am I in the place of God? You intended to harm me, but God intended it for good to accomplish what is now being done, the saving of many lives. So then, **do not be afraid**. I will provide for you and your children." He reassured them and spoke kindly to them.*

Exodus 14:13-14—*Moses answered the people, "**Do not be afraid**. Stand firm and you will see the deliverance the Lord will bring you today. The Egyptians you see today you will never see again. The Lord will fight for you; you need only to be still."*

Exodus 20:20-21—*(After receiving the Ten Commandments) Moses said to the people, "**Do not be afraid**. God has come to test you, so that the fear of God will be with you to keep you from sinning." The people remained at a distance, while Moses approached the thick darkness where God was.*

Numbers 14:8-9—*"If the Lord is pleased with us, he will lead us into that land, a land flowing with milk and honey, and will give it to us. Only do not rebel against the Lord. And **do not be afraid** of the people of the land, because we will swallow them up. Their protection is gone, but the Lord is wIth us. **Do not be afraid** of them."*

Numbers 21:34-35—*The Lord said to Moses, "**Do not be afraid**, for I have handed Og king of Bashan over to you, with his whole army and his land. Do to him what you did to Sihon king of the Amorites, who reigned in Heshbon." So they struck him down, together with his sons and his whole army, leaving them no survivors. And they took possession of his land.*

Deuteronomy 1:21—*(And Moses said to the people of Israel)"See, the Lord your God has given you the land. Go up and take possession of it as the Lord, the God of your fathers told you. **Do not be afraid**; do not be discouraged."*

Deuteronomy 3:2—*(And Moses said to the people of Israel)"The Lord said to me, '**Do not be afraid**, for I have handed Og the king of Bashan over to you with his whole army and his land. Do to him what you did to Sihon king of the Amorites, who reigned in Heshbon.'"*

Deuteronomy 3:21-22—*(And Moses said to the people of Israel)"You have seen with your own eyes all that the Lord your God has done to these two kings. The Lord will do the same to all the kingdoms over there where you are going. **Do not be afraid**; the Lord your God himself will fight for you."*

Deuteronomy 20:1-4—*When you go to war against your enemies and see horses and chariots and an army greater than yours, **do not be afraid**, because the Lord your God, who brought you up out of Egypt, will be with you. When you are about to go into battle the priest shall come forward and address the army. He shall say: "Hear, O Israel, today you are going into battle against your enemies. Do not be fainthearted and **do not be afraid**; do not be terrified or give way to panic before them. For the Lord your God is the one who goes with you to fight for you against your enemies to give you victory."*

Deuteronomy 31:6—*(And Moses said to the people of Israel)"Be strong and courageous. **Do not be afraid** and do not be terrified because of them, for the Lord your God goes with you; He will never leave you nor forsake you."*

Deuteronomy 31:7-8—*Then Moses summoned Joshua and said to him in the presence of all Israel, "Be strong and courageous, for you must go with this people into the land that the Lord swore to their forefathers to give them, and you must divide it among them as the inheritance. The Lord Himself goes before you and will be with you; He will never leave you nor forsake you. **Do not be afraid**, do not be discouraged."*

Joshua 8:1—*Then the Lord said to Joshua, "**Do not be afraid**; do not be discouraged. Take the whole army with you, and go up and attack Ai. For I have delivered into your hands the king of Ai, his people, his city and his land."*

Joshua 10:8—*So Joshua marched up from Gilgal with his entire army, including all the best fighting men. The Lord said to Joshua, "**Do not be afraid**; for I have given them into your hand. Not one of them will be able to withstand you."*

Joshua 10:25-26—*Joshua said to them, "**Don't be afraid**; do not be discouraged. Be strong and courageous. This is what the Lord will do to all the enemies you are going to fight." Then Joshua struck and killed the five kings of the Amorites and hung them on trees, and they were left hanging on the trees until evening.*

Judges 4:18-21—*Jael went out to meet Sisera and said to him, "Come, my lord, come right in. **Don't be afraid.**" So he entered her tent, and she put a covering over him...But Jael, Heber's wife, picked up a tent peg and a hammer and went quietly to him while he lay fast asleep, exhausted. She drove the peg through his temple into the ground, and he died.*

Judges 6:7-10—*When the Israelites cried to the Lord because of Midian, He sent them a prophet, who said: "This is what the Lord, the God of Israel says: I brought you up out of Egypt, out of the land of slavery. I snatched you from the power of Egypt and from the hand of all your oppressors. I drove them from before you and gave you their land. I said to you, 'I am the Lord your God; **do not be afraid** of the gods of the Amorites, in whose land you live.' But you have not listened to me."*

Judges 6:23--*But the Lord said to Gideon, "Peace! **Fear not**. You are not going to die."*

Ruth 3:11-12—*(Boaz said to Ruth)"And now, my daughter, **do not be afraid**. I will do for you all you ask. All my fellow townsmen know that you are a woman of noble character. Although it is true that I am near of kin, there is a kinsman-redeemer nearer that I."*

1 Samuel 4:19-21—*(Samuel's) daughter-in-law, the wife of Phinehas was pregnant and near the time of delivery. When she heard the news that the ark of God had been captured and that her father-in-law and her husband were dead, she went into labor and gave birth, but she was overcome by her labor pains. As she was dying, the women attending her said, "**Do not be afraid**, you have given birth to a son." But she did not respond or pay any attention. She named the boy Ichabod, saying, "The glory has departed from Israel."*

1 Samuel 12:19-20—*The people all said to Samuel, "Pray to the Lord your God for your servants so that we will not die, for we have added to all our other sins the evil of asking for a king." "**Do not be afraid**," Samuel replied. "You have done all this evil; yet do not turn away from the Lord, but serve the Lord with all your heart."*

1 Samuel 22:20-23—*But Abiathar, escaped and fled to join David. He told David that Saul had killed the priests of the Lord. Then David said to Abiathar: "That day, when Doeg the Edomite was there, I knew he would be sure to tell Saul. I am responsible for the death of your father's whole family. Stay with me;* **do not be afraid**; *the man who is seeking your life is seeking mine also. You will be safe with me."*

1 Samuel 23:15-17—*While David was at Horesh in the Desert of Ziph, he learned that Saul had come out to take his life. And Saul's son Jonathan went to David at Horesh and helped him find strength in God.* '**Do not be afraid**," *he said. "My father Saul will not lay a hand on you. You will be king over Israel, and I will be second to you. Even my father Saul knows this."*

2 Samuel 9:7—"**Do not be afraid**," *David said (to Mephibosheth), "For I will surely show you kindness for the sake of your father, Jonathan. I will restore to you all the land that belonged to your grandfather Saul, and you will always eat at my table."*

2 Samuel 13:28—*Absalom ordered his men, "Listen! When Amnon is in high spirits from drinking wine and I say to you, 'Strike Amnon down,' then kill him.* **Do not be afraid**. *Have I not given you this order? Be strong and brave."*

1 Kings 17:13-14—*Elijah said to (the Widow at Zarephath), "***Do not be afraid**. *Go home and do as you have said. But first make a small cake of bread for me from what you have and bring it to me and then make something for yourself and your son. For this is what the Lord, the God of Israel says: 'The jar of flour will not be used up and the jug of oil will not run dry until the day the Lord gives rain on the land.'"*

2 Kings 6:15-16—*When the servant (of Elisha) got up and went out early the next morning, an army with horses and chariots had surrounded the city. "Oh, my lord, what shall we do?" the servant asked. "***Do not be afraid**," *Elisha answered. "Those who are with us are more than those who are with them."*

2 Kings 25:22-24—*Nebuchadnezzar king of Babylon appointed Gedaliah son of Ahikam, to be over the people he had left behind in Judah. Gedaliah took an oath to reassure them and their men. "***Do not be afraid** *of the Babylonian officials," he said. "Settle down in the land and serve the king of Babylon, and it will go well with you."*

1 Chronicles 28:20—*David also said to Solomon his son, "Be strong and courageous, and do the work.* **Do not be afraid**; *do not be discouraged, for the Lord God, my God is with you. He will not fail you or forsake you until all the work for the service of the temple of the Lord is finished."*

2 Chronicles 20:15-17—*(Jahaziel son of Zechariah) said, "Listen, King Jehoshaphat and all who live in Judah and Jerusalem! This is what the Lord says to you: "***Do not be afraid**; *do not be discouraged because of this vast army. For the battle is not yours, but God's. Tomorrow march down against them. You will not have to fight this battle. Take up your positions; stand firm and see the deliverance the Lord will give you, O Judah and Jerusalem.* **Do not be afraid**; *do not be discouraged. Go out to face them tomorrow, and the Lord will be with you."*

Job 11:15—*(Zophar the Naamathite said to Job) "Yet if you devote your heart to him and stretch out your hands to him, if you put away the sin that is in your hand and allow no evil to dwell in your tent, then you will lift up your face without shame; you will stand firm **and will not be afraid.**"*

Psalm 27:1-3—*The Lord is my light and my salvation—whom shall I fear? The Lord is the stronghold of my life—of whom shall I be afraid? When evil men advance against me to devour my flesh, when my enemies and my foes attack me, they will stumble and fall. Though an army besiege me, **my heart will not be afraid**; though war break out against me, even then will I be confident.*

Psalm 118:1-6—*Give thanks to the Lord, for He is good; His love endures forever. Let Israel say: "His love endures forever." Let the house of Aaron say: "His love endures forever." Let those who fear the Lord say: "His love endures forever." In my anguish I cried to the Lord, and He answered me; **I will not be afraid**. What can man do to me?*

Proverbs 3:25—***Have no fear*** *of sudden disaster or of the ruin that overtakes the wicked, for the Lord will be your confidence and will keep your foot from being snared.*

Isaiah 7:3-4—*Then the Lord said to Isaiah, "Go out, you and your son Shear-Jashub, to meet Ahaz. Say to him, 'Be careful, keep calm and **don't be afraid**. Do not lose heart because of these two smoldering stubs of fireweed—the fierce anger of Rezin and Aram.'"*

Isaiah 35:4—*Say to those with fearful hearts, "Be strong, **do not fear**; your God will come with vengeance; with divine retribution He will come to save you."*

Isaiah 41:10-13—*"**Do not be afraid**, for I am with you; do not be dismayed, for I am your God. I will strengthen you and help you; I will uphold you with my righteous right hand. For I am the Lord, your God, who takes hold of your right hand and says to you, '**Do not fear**; I will help you. **Do not be afraid**, O worm Jacob, O little Israel, for I myself will help you,' declares the Lord, your Redeemer, the Holy One of Israel."*

Isaiah 43:5—*"**Do not be afraid**, for I am with you; I will bring your children from the east and gather you from the west."*

Isaiah 44:2-3—*This is what the Lord says—He who made you, who formed you in the womb, and who will help you: **Do not be afraid**, O Jacob, my servant, Jeshurun, whom I have chosen. For I will pour water on the thirsty land, and streams on the dry ground; I will pour out my Spirit on your offspring, and my blessing on your descendants."*

Isaiah 44:8—*"Do not tremble, **do not be afraid**. Did I not proclaim this and foretell it long ago? You are my witnesses. Is there any God besides me? No, there is no other Rock; I know not one."*

Isaiah 51:7—*"Hear me, you who know what is right, you people who have my law in your hearts: **do not fear** the reproach of men or be terrified by their insults."*

Isaiah 54:4—*"**Do not be afraid**; you will not suffer shame. **Do not fear** disgrace; you will not be humiliated. You will forget the shame of your youth and remember no more the reproach of your widowhood."*

Isaiah 54:14—*"In righteousness you will be established: Tyranny will be far from you; **you will have nothing to fear**. Terror will be far removed, it will not come near you."*

Jeremiah 23:4—*"I will place shepherds over them who will tend them, **and they will no longer be afraid** or terrified, nor will any be missing," declares the Lord.*

Jeremiah 30:8-10—*"In that day," declares the Lord Almighty, "I will break the yoke off their necks and will tear off their bonds; no longer will foreigners enslave them. Instead, they will serve the Lord their God and David their king, whom I will raise up for them. **So do not fear**, O Jacob my servant; do not be dismayed, O Israel."*

Jeremiah 40:9—*Gedaliah son of Ahikam, took an oath to reassure them and their men. "**Do not be afraid** to serve the Babylonians," he said. "Settle down in the land and serve the king of Babylon, and it will go well with you. I myself will stay at Mizpah to represent you before the Babylonians who come to us, but you are to harvest the wine, summer fruit and oil, and put them in your storage jars, and live in the towns you have taken over."*

Jeremiah 46:27-28—*"**Do not fear**, O Jacob my servant; do not be dismayed, O Israel. I will surely save you out of a distant place, your descendants from the land of their exile. Jacob will again have peace and security, and no one will make him afraid. **Do not fear**, O Jacob my servant, for I am with you," declares the Lord. "Though I completely destroy all the nations among which I scatter you, I will not completely destroy you. I will discipline you but only with justice; I will not let you go entirely unpunished."*

Lamentations 3:55-58—*I called on your name, O Lord, from the depths of the pit. You heard my plea: "Do not close your ears to my cry for relief." You came near when I called you, and you said, "**Do not fear**." O Lord, you took up my case; you redeemed my life.*

Daniel 10:10-12—*A hand touched me and set me trembling on my hands and knees. The man dressed in linen said, "Daniel, you who are highly esteemed, consider carefully the words I am about to speak to you, and stand up, for I have been sent to you." And when he said this to me, I stood up trembling. Then he continued, "**Do not be afraid**, Daniel. Since the first day that you set your mind to gain understanding and to humble yourself before your God, your words were heard, and I have come in response to them."*

Joel 2:21-22—*"**Be not afraid**, O land; be glad and rejoice. Surely the Lord has done great things. **Be not afraid**, O wild animals, for the open pastures are becoming green. The trees are bearing their fruit; the fig tree and the vine yield their riches."*

Zephaniah 3:16-17—*"On that day they will say to Jerusalem, '**Do not fear**, O Zion; do not let your hands hang limp. The Lord your God is with you, He is mighty to save. He will take great delight in you, He will quiet you with His love, He will rejoice over you with singing.'"*

Haggai 2:4-5—*"Be strong, all you people of the land," declares the Lord, "and work. For I am with you," declares the Lord Almighty. "This is what I covenanted with you when you came out of Egypt. And my Spirit remains among you.* **Do not fear.***"*

Zechariah 8:13—*"As you have been an object of cursing among the nations, O Judah and Israel, so will I save you, and you will be a blessing.* **Do not be afraid***, but let your hands be strong."*

Zechariah 8:14-15—*This is what the Lord Almighty says: "Just as I had determined to bring disaster upon you and showed no pity when your fathers angered me," says the Lord Almighty, "so now I have determined to do good again to Jerusalem and Judah.* **Do not be afraid.***"*

Matthew 1:18-21—*This is how the birth of Jesus Christ came about: His mother Mary was pledged to be married to Joseph, but before they came together, she was found to be with child through the Holy Spirit. Because Joseph her husband was a righteous man and did not want to expose her to public disgrace, he had in mind to divorce her quietly. But after he had considered this, an angel of the Lord appeared to him in a dream and said, "Joseph son of David,* **do not be afraid** *to take Mary home as your wife, because what is conceived in her is from the Holy Spirit. She will give birth to a son, and you are to give him the name Jesus, because He will save his people from their sins."*

Matthew 10:28—*"***Do not be afraid** *of those who kill the body but cannot kill the soul. Rather,* **be afraid** *of the One who can destroy both soul and body in hell."*

Matthew 10:29-31—*"Are not two sparrows sold for a penny? Yet not one of them will fall to the ground apart from the will of your Father. And even the very hairs of your head are all numbered. So* **don't be afraid***; you are worth more than many sparrows."*

Matthew 28:1-6—*After the Sabbath, at dawn on the first day of the week, Mary Magdalene and the other Mary went to look at the tomb. There was a violent earthquake, for an angel of the Lord came down from heaven and, going to the tomb, rolled back the stone and sat on it. His appearance was like lightning, and his clothes were white as snow. The guards were so afraid of him that they shook and became like dead men. The angel said to the women, "***Do not be afraid***, for I know that you are looking for Jesus, who was crucified. He is not here; He has risen."*

Luke 1:11-13—*Then an angel of the Lord appeared, standing at the right side of the altar of incense. When Zechariah saw him, he was startled and was gripped with fear. But the angel said to him:* **Do not be afraid***, Zechariah; your prayer has been heard. Your wife Elizabeth will bear you a son, and you are to give him the name John."*

Luke 1:26-31—*In the sixth month, God sent the angel Gabriel to Nazareth, a town in Galilee, to a virgin pledged to be married to a man named Joseph, a descendant of David. The virgin's name was Mary. The angel went to her and said, "Greetings, you who are highly favored! The Lord is with you." Mary was greatly troubled at his words and wondered what kind of greeting this might be. But the angel said to her, "***Do not be afraid***, Mary, you have found favor with God. You will be with child and give birth to a son, and you are to give Him the name Jesus."*

Luke 2:8-12—*And there were shepherds living out in the fields nearby, keeping watch over their flocks at night. An angel of the Lord appeared to them, and the glory of the Lord shone around them, and they were terrified. But the angel said to them, "**Do not be afraid**. I bring you good news of great joy that will be for all the people. Today in the town of David a Savior has been born to you; He is Christ the Lord. This will be a sign to you: You will find a baby wrapped in cloths and lying in a manger."*

Luke 5:8-11—*When Simon Peter saw (all the fish in the net) he fell at Jesus' knees and said, "Go away from me, Lord; I am a sinful man!" For he and all his companions were astonished at the catch of fish they had taken, and so were James and John, the sons of Zebedee, Simon's partners. Then Jesus said to Simon, "**Don't be afraid**; from now on you will catch men." So they pulled their boats up on shore, left everything and followed Him.*

Luke 8:49-50—*While Jesus was still speaking, someone came from the house of Jairus, the synagogue ruler. "Your daughter is dead," he said. "Don't bother the teacher anymore." Hearing this, Jesus said to Jairus, "**Don't be afraid**; just believe, and she will be healed."*

Luke 12:4-7—*"I tell you, my friends, **do not be afraid** of those who kill the body and after that can do no more. But I will show you whom you should fear: Fear him who, after the killing of the body, has power to throw you into hell. Yes, I tell you, fear him. Are not five sparrows sold for two pennies? Yet not one of them is forgotten by God. Indeed, the very hairs of your head are all numbered. **Don't be afraid**; you are worth more than many sparrows."*

Luke 12:32-34—*"**Do not be afraid**, little flock, for your Father has been pleased to give you the kingdom. Sell your possessions and give to the poor. Provide purses for yourselves that will not wear out, a treasure in heaven that will not be exhausted, where no thief comes near and no moth destroys. For where your treasure is, there your heart will be also."*

John 12:12-15—*The next day the great crowd that had come for the Passover Feast heard that Jesus was on his way to Jerusalem. They took palm branches and went out to meet Him, shouting, "Hosanna!" "Blessed is he who comes in the name of the Lord!" "Blessed is the King of Israel!" Jesus found a young donkey and sat upon it, as it is written, "**Do not be afraid**, O Daughter of Zion; see, your king is coming, seated on a donkey's colt." (Zechariah 9:9)*

Acts 27:21-24—*After the men had gone a long time without food, Paul stood up before them and said: "Men, you should have taken my advice not to sail from Crete; then you would have spared yourselves this damage and loss. But now I urge you to keep up your courage, because not one of you will be lost; only the ship will be destroyed. Last night an angel of the God whose I am and whom I serve stood beside me and said, '**Do not be afraid**, Paul. You must stand trial before Caesar; and God has graciously given you the lives of all who sail with you.'"*

Hebrews 13:5-6—*"Keep your lives free from the love of money and be content with what you have, because God has said, "Never will I leave you; never will I forsake you." So we say with confidence, "The Lord is my helper; **I will not be afraid**. What can man do to me?"*

Revelation 1:17—*"When I saw (the Son of Man), I fell at his feet as though dead. Then He placed His right hand on me and said: "**Do not be afraid**, I am the First and the Last. I am the Living One; I was dead, and behold I am alive for ever and ever! And I hold the keys of death and Hades."*

Revelation 2:10—*"**Do not be afraid** of what you are about to suffer. I tell you, the devil will put some of you in prison to test you, and you will suffer persecution for ten days. Be faithful, even to the point of death, and I will give you the crown of life."*

From Genesis to Revelation

Genesis 15:1 (NIV)

"Do not be afraid. I am your shield."

Revelation 2:10 (NIV)

"Do not be afraid of what you are about suffer."

My Favorite "Fear not"

The Lord is my Light and my Salvation

Whom shall I fear?

The Lord is the Stronghold of my life

Of whom shall I be afraid?

When evil men advance against me

To devour my flesh,

When my enemies and foes attack me.

They will stumble and fall.

Though an army besiege me,

My heart will not fear;

Though war break out against me,

Even then will I be content.

One thing I ask of the Lord,

This is what I seek:

That I may dwell in the house of the Lord

All the days of my life.

Psalm 27:1-4 (NIV)

Author's Note

I would like to take a moment to tell you about my Best Friend, Jesus.

I was raised in a Christian home and accepted Jesus as my Savior at an early age during a Kids Crusade at our church. I have served Him all of my life.

I used to think that meant I didn't have a testimony. I was not saved from a life of drugs. I was not raised in an abusive home. I had kind and loving parents. I attended church almost every week of my life.

But I know now that every day is the day of salvation and my Best Friend keeps me from a life of sin by helping me make wise decisions. Sometimes I don't make the best choices, but He is always there to forgive me.

The most important thing is; I am not alone. I do not have to go through trials alone. I can call on Him *any time*, day or night.

If you are interested in having a Best Friend like that, let me share the *Romans Roadmap* with you.

If we are honest with ourselves, we will admit that we all make mistakes. None of us is perfect. The Bible addresses this very thing when it says, **"For all have sinned, and come short of the glory of God."** Romans 3:23 (NIV).

And what happens when we continue to do bad things? Our life becomes a mess. We are miserable and life is not worth living. **"For the wages of sin is death; but the gift of God is eternal life through Jesus Christ our Lord."** Romans 6:23 (NIV).

There's my Best Friend, Jesus. And He will come to you if **"you confess with your mouth that Jesus is Lord, and believe in your heart that God raised Him from the dead— you will be saved."** Romans 10:9 (NIV)

How would you like to have peace in your life and in your heart? **"Therefore, since we have been justified through faith, we have peace with God through our Lord Jesus Christ."** Romans 5:1 (NIV).

It seems like my Best Friend Jesus is in every verse, doesn't it? That is because He left His home in Heaven to come down to this earth and die on the cross for our sins. And if you accept Him, He will set you free.

I ask you to join me in this prayer:

Heavenly Father,

*I come to you in prayer
asking for the forgiveness of my sins.
I confess with my mouth
and believe with my heart that Jesus is your Son,
and that He died on the cross at Calvary
that I might be forgiven
and have eternal life
in the kingdom of Heaven.*

*Father, I believe that Jesus rose from the dead
and I ask you right now to come in to my life
and be my personal Lord and Savior.
I repent of my sins
and will worship you all the days of my life!
Because your Word Is truth,
I confess with my mouth
that I am born again
and cleansed by the blood of Jesus.*

In Jesus' name,

Amen

Those important verses from the *Romans Roadmap* were all taken from the Book of Romans in the New Testament of the Bible. There are many more helpful verses in there.

But first of all, I would encourage you to read the entire Book of John. This will tell you of Jesus' life on earth and what He did to save us from ourselves.

I would also recommend that you find a Bible-believing church in your neighborhood and go fellowship with others who have been set free.

For many more answers and good advice on what to do with your newfound life, go online to the sites www.journeyanswers.org or www.whojesusis.org.

And if you would like to know how many other people around the world have made and are making the same decision you just did, go to www.project100million.org and look for the live map showing new Christians being born again every 80 seconds.

God Bless You,

Tami J.